CONTENTS

INTRODUCTION

This book is written, primarily, for child care workers and students. It is particularly relevant for students studying for the Diploma in Nursery Nursing, the Certificate in Child Care and Education, the BTEC National Diploma in Early Childhood Studies and food hygiene courses.

Most people know what constitutes a healthy, balanced diet for adults, but different principles apply when providing food and drink for children. A sound knowledge of nutrition and its importance in the health, growth and development of children is necessary for child care workers. High standards of hygiene in storing and preparing food also play a major role in keeping children healthy.

The first two chapters provide the essential knowledge needed to understand nutrients and their specific functions, as well as the foods which form the basis of a well-balanced diet. You may find it useful to read these two chapters first.

After the first two chapters there are activities for you to complete. These are designed to help you to link your theory and practical work. Keep all your written work for inclusion in your portfolio which will provide evidence of prior learning for your National Vocational Qualification assessment. This evidence may also be useful for entry to other child care courses or for presentation at an interview. A list of useful addresses and a glossary are at the back of the book.

We hope you will find this book helpful.

A PRACTICAL GUIDE TO CHILD NUTRITION

City College
NORWICH

Angela Dare
Margaret O'Donovan

Stanley Thornes (Publishers) Ltd

First published in 1996 by:
Stanley Thornes (Publishers) Ltd
Delta Place
27 Bath Road
CHELTENHAM
GL53 7TH
United Kingdom

00 / 10 9 8 7 6 5 4

A catalogue record for this book is available from the British Library.
ISBN 0 7487 2375 7

Typeset by Columns Design Ltd, Reading
Printed and bound in Great Britain by T.J. International, Padstow, Cornwall

ABOUT THE AUTHORS

Angela Dare has a background in health visiting and teaching, and is currently Co-ordinator of CACHE Courses at City and Islington College, London (formerly North London College).

Margaret O'Donovan has a background in nursery nursing, midwifery and health visiting, and teaches at Chiltern Nursery Training College, Caversham.

The authors have worked together for many years teaching students on child care courses at City and Islington College. Both were examiners for the NNEB. Angela Dare is an External Moderator for CACHE.

They are authors of *A Practical Guide to Working with Babies* (ISBN 0 7487 1743 9), also published by Stanley Thornes.

ACKNOWLEDGEMENTS

The authors would like to give special thanks to Aaquib, Camilla, Laura, Jordan and Sanna for allowing their photographs to be reproduced or used as references for the artist.

The authors and publishers are also grateful to the following for permission to reproduce material:

Tables 1.2 and 1.3, pages 7 and 8, © Crown, reproduced from MAFF, *The Manual of Nutrition*, tenth edition (HMSO, 1995) by permission of the Controller of Her Majesty's Stationery Office.

Percentile charts, page 117, © Child Growth Foundation (address page 145). The full range of nine percentile charts produced for the UK are obtainable from Harlow Printing, Maxwell Street, South Shields NE33 4PU.

Cover photograph, Format/Judy Harrison.

1 NUTRITION

To help your understanding of the terminology used in nutrition we have used the first part of this chapter to explain commonly used words and phrases. You will hear them used by your teachers and read them as you progress through the other chapters of the book.

The tables on pages 7 and 8 will be useful when you prepare infant feeds and weaning foods, plan and prepare meals for children, and help them with shopping and cooking activities.

Definitions and terms

NUTRITION

Nutrition is the study of food and how it is used in the body.

FOOD

Food is any solid or liquid that nourishes the body by:
- providing warmth and energy to maintain body temperature and keep all organs and muscles working properly
- providing new material for growth. This includes tissue for the brain and nervous system; organs such as the heart, liver, lungs and kidneys; muscle and bone structures; and the lining of the gut, lungs and blood vessels
- maintaining and renewing body tissues
- keeping all the body processes, including the prevention of infection, in good order.

Habits, cultural patterns and family attitudes to food affect the variety and types of food eaten by children.

NUTRIENTS

Nutrients are the 'building blocks' of food which carry out the above functions. There are seven essential nutrients: proteins, carbohydrates, fats, vitamins, minerals, fibre and water. They each have a particular part to play in the growth and health of the body.

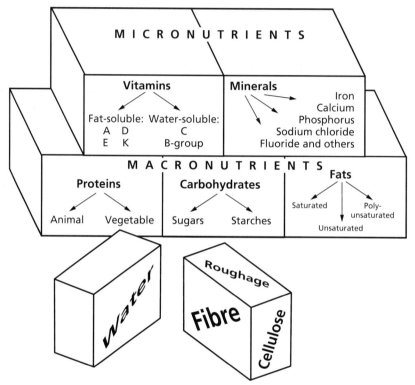

The essential nutritional building blocks

MACRONUTRIENTS

Proteins, fats and carbohydrates are known as macronutrients. They have many different functions but they **all provide energy**. They are needed in relatively **large** amounts by the body and are measured in grams.

MICRONUTRIENTS

Vitamins and minerals are known as micronutrients. They do not supply energy and are needed in relatively **small** amounts by the body. They are measured in milligrams or micrograms.

ENERGY

Energy is the ability to do work. Just as a car needs petrol (energy) to make it go, so our bodies need food to produce the energy to keep us warm, active and healthy. Even during sleep, energy is needed to keep the heart pumping and all the other organs functioning normally. Importantly, children also need energy for **growth**. Most foods provide some energy, but the main suppliers are the **macronutrients**. The energy produced by food is released slowly into the body and is controlled by substances called enzymes.

MEASUREMENT OF ENERGY

The international measurement unit of energy (including food energy) is the **joule**. However, the older term **calorie** is more commonly recognised and used in the UK, and is the one used throughout this book.

The joule and the calorie are small units, so the terms **kilojoule** (1000 joules) and **kilocalorie** (1000 calories) are used by the Department of Health in the table of Estimated Average Requirements for energy (see page 7) and on the nutritional labels of packaged foods.

4.2 kilojoules (kJ) = 1 kilocalorie (kcal)

1 g protein	provides	17 kJ/4 kcal
1 g fat	provides	37 kJ/9 kcal
1 g carbohydrate	provides	16 kJ/4 kcal

See Table 1.1 on page 7.

ENERGY REQUIREMENTS

Energy requirements vary according to age, gender and the amount of physical activity a person undertakes. People engaged in heavy physical work need more energy than office workers. Women tend to need less energy than men, although during pregnancy and lactation their energy requirements increase. Children and adolescents need a lot of energy because they are growing and active.

DIETARY REFERENCE VALUES (DRVs)

These were published in 1991 by the Department of Health. They replace the former Recommended Daily Amounts (RDAs). DRVs refer to a range of daily nutrient requirements for different groups of individuals. They provide a guide when planning diets. There are three levels of intake:
■ **Estimated Average Requirement** (EAR). This gives the **average** require-

ment for food energy or nutrient intake. Some people will need more and some less than this recommendation.

■ **Reference Nutrient Intake** (RNI). This refers to the level of nutrient intake sufficient for almost every individual, even those with high nutritional requirements. These intakes will prevent nutritional disorders and, in children, promote normal growth.

■ **Lower Reference Nutrient Intake** (LRNI). This is the amount set for the few individuals who have the lowest nutritional needs. Anyone constantly eating less than the LRNI will almost certainly become deficient in that nutrient.

It is important that energy intake (calories) is neither excessive nor inadequate for individual needs so the recommendation for the different groups is set at the EAR.

See Tables 1.2 and 1.3 on pages 7 and 8. These tables will be useful guides when you are planning children's meals.

ENZYMES

Enzymes are special proteins needed for all the chemical reactions which take place in the body. Digestive enzymes, or juices, are made by the body in the salivary glands (in the mouth), and in the stomach, liver, pancreas and intestinal glands.

METABOLISM

This word is used to describe all the changes that take place in the body to do with food and the use of energy.

COMMITTEE ON MEDICAL ASPECTS OF FOOD POLICY (COMA)

COMA is an independent committee of experts in the fields of nutrition and health. One of its standing committees is the Panel on Child Nutrition which reviews and considers aspects of children's nutrition. In 1994 it prepared a report, including recommendations, called 'Weaning and the Weaning Diet' (HMSO, 1994).

NATIONAL ADVISORY COMMITTEE ON NUTRITION EDUCATION (NACNE)

NACNE is made up of experienced nutritionists who produce guidelines on nutrition policy aimed at improving the health of the nation.

The human alimentary and digestive system

The alimentary canal is a long muscular tube through which food passes. It is made up of the mouth, the oesophagus (gullet), the stomach, the small and large intestines, the rectum and the anus. Digestive juices are secreted into the alimentary canal to break up and digest food ready for absorption into the blood stream.

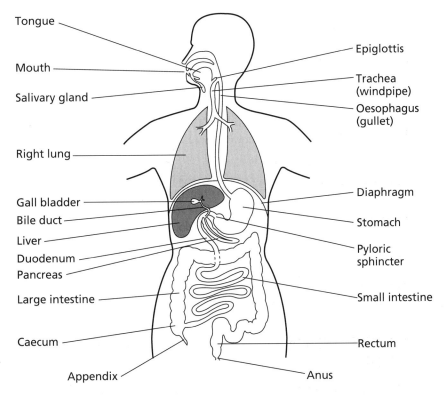

The human alimentary system

WHAT HAPPENS TO FOOD WHEN WE EAT IT?

In the mouth
Chewing breaks the food into small pieces. At the same time, it is mixed with saliva from the salivary glands to form a bolus (soft mass of chewed food) which is then swallowed. Swallowing pushes the food down the oesophagus into the stomach.

In the stomach
Food is changed and partly digested by the action of gastric juices. It then

leaves the stomach through the pyloric sphincter (a ring of muscle) which is normally closed but opens at intervals to let the food through, a little at a time, into the small intestine.

In the small intestine
Further digestion takes place here as digestive juices from the pancreas, gall bladder and intestine are mixed with the food. The food is then absorbed into the body through the walls of the small intestine. Materials remaining after absorption pass into the large intestine.

In the large intestine
The material here is mainly water, fibre and bacteria. Water and any useful substances remaining from food residue are absorbed. The remainder (fibre, dead cells and bacteria) form the faeces. Peristaltic action moves the faeces into the rectum and out of the body via the anus.

(Peristalsis: Wave-like contraction and relaxation movements of the small and large intestines which help the digestion and absorption of food and the expulsion of faeces from the body.)

How food energy is produced in the body

CARBOHYDRATES

Carbohydrates (sugars and starches) are absorbed into the body as glucose. Glucose provides the body with energy. Some glucose circulates in the blood stream to provide instant energy. Most is stored in the liver and muscles as **glycogen** which can be broken down as necessary and converted back into glucose for use by the body as energy. Excess glucose is stored as fat in the fatty tissue of the body.

FATS

Fats are absorbed into the body as fatty acids and glycerol. These are used by the body to provide, among other things, energy for warmth and work. Those not required for immediate 'fuel' are stored as fatty tissue which can be converted into energy as necessary.

PROTEIN

Excess protein *cannot* be stored in the body so, once its main functions have been carried out, any that is left over is converted into:
- energy for immediate use or stored energy in the form of glycogen or fat
- urea, a waste product which is excreted by the kidneys.

Table 1.1 Measurements used for food and nutrition

Energy

joule = J	1000 J = 1 kJ
kilojoule = kJ	4.2 kJ = 1 kcal
megajoule = MJ	1000 kJ = 1 MJ
kilocalorie = kcal	

Weight

microgram = µg	1 000 000 µg = 1 g
milligram = mg	1000 µg = 1 mg
gram = g	1000 mg = 1 g
kilogram = kg	1000 g = 1 kg
ounce = oz	16 oz = 1 lb
pound = lb	
	28 g = 1 oz
	100 g = 3.5 oz
	454 g = 1 lb
	1 kg = 2.2 lb

Liquid measure

fluid ounce = fl. oz	1000 ml = 1 l
pint = pt	
	20 fl.oz = 1 pt
millilitre = ml	
litre = l	28 ml = 1 fl.oz
	568 ml = 1 pt
	1 l = 1.75 pt

Table 1.2 Estimated Average Requirements for energy in the UK (per day)

Age range	Males		Females	
	MJ	kcal	MJ	kcal
0–3 months (formula fed)	2.28	545	2.16	515
4–6 months	2.89	690	2.69	645
7–9 months	3.44	825	3.20	765
10–12 months	3.85	920	3.61	865
1–3 years	5.15	1230	4.86	1165
4–6 years	7.16	1715	6.46	1545
7–10 years	8.24	1970	7.28	1740
11–14 years	9.27	2220	7.92	1845
15–18 years	11.51	2755	8.83	2110
19–50 years	10.60	2550	8.10	1940
51–59 years	10.60	2550	8.00	1900
60–64 years	9.93	2380	7.99	1900
65–74 years	9.71	2330	7.96	1900
75+ years	8.77	2100	7.61	1810
Pregnant*			+0.80	+200
Lactating				
1 month			+1.90	+450
2 months			+2.20	+530
3 months			+2.40	+570
4–6 months			+2.00	+480
>6 months			+1.00	+240

* Last trimester only

Table 1.3 Reference Nutrient Intakes for selected nutrients for the UK (per day)

Age range	Protein (g)	Calcium (mg)	Iron (mg)	Zinc (mg)	Vitamin A (µg)	Thiamin (mg)	Vitamin B₆ (mg)[a]	Folic acid (µg)	Vitamin C (mg)
0–3 months (formula fed)	12.5	525	1.7	4.0	350	0.2	0.2	50	25
4–6 months	12.7	525	4.3	4.0	350	0.2	0.2	50	25
7–9 months	13.7	525	7.8	5.0	350	0.2	0.3	50	25
10–12 months	14.9	525	7.8	5.0	350	0.3	0.4	50	25
1–3 years	14.5	350	6.9	5.0	400	0.5	0.7	70	30
4–6 years	19.7	450	6.1	6.5	500	0.7	0.9	100	30
7–10 years	28.3	550	8.7	7.0	500	0.7	1.0	150	30
Males									
11–14 years	42.1	1000	11.3	9.0	600	0.9	1.2	200	35
15–18 years	55.2	1000	11.3	9.5	700	1.1	1.5	200	40
19–50 years	55.5	700	8.7	9.5	700	1.0	1.4	200	40
50+ years	53.3	700	8.7	9.5	700	0.9	1.4	200	40
Females									
11–14 years	41.2	800	14.8[b]	9.0	600	0.7	1.0	200	35
15–18 years	45.0	800	14.8[b]	7.0	600	0.8	1.2	200	40
19–50 years	45.0	700	14.8[b]	7.0	600	0.8	1.2	200	40
50+ years	46.5	700	8.7	7.0	600	0.8	1.2	200	40
Pregnant	+6.0	c	c	c	+100	+0.1[d]	c	+100	+10
Lactating:									
0–4 months	+11.0	+550	c	+6.0	+350	+0.2	c	+60	+30
over 4 months	+8.0	+550	c	+2.5	+350	+0.2	c	+60	+30

a Based on protein providing 14.7 per cent of the EAR for energy.
b These RNIs will not meet the needs of approximately 10 per cent of women with the highest menstrual losses, who may need iron supplements.
c No increment.
d Last trimester only.

QUICK CHECK

1 What are:
   a) nutrients?
   b) macronutrients?
   c) micronutrients?
2 a) What is energy?
   b) How is it measured?
3 How is energy used in the body?
4 Why do children need a lot of energy?
5 What do you understand by the following terms:
   a) Dietary Reference Values?
   b) Reference Nutrient Intake?
6 a) What are enzymes?
   b) Where in the body are digestive enzymes made?
7 In which part of the intestine does absorption of food take place?
8 What is peristalsis?
9 What is the end product of carbohydrate digestion?
10 a) What is glycogen?
   b) Where in the body is it stored?
11 How is excess glucose stored in the body?
12 What happens to excess protein in the body?
13 Name the seven essential nutrients.
14 How many grams are there in:
   a) one ounce?
   b) one pound?
15 How many millilitres are there in:
   a) one fluid ounce?
   b) one pint?

KEY WORDS AND TERMS

You need to know what these words and phrases mean. Go back through the chapter and find out.

food	calorie
nutrients	Dietary Reference Values
macronutrients	enzymes
micronutrients	metabolism
energy	COMA
joule	glycogen

2 *THE ESSENTIAL NUTRIENTS*

> **This chapter covers:**
> ■ The role of the essential nutrients
> ■ The food groups
> ■ Dairy, staple and fortified foods

The role of the essential nutrients

Information about the seven essential nutrients is set out in the charts on pages 17–23, and in Tables 2.1 and 2.2 on pages 24–7. Try to read these frequently, together with the text below – this will help you to gain a thorough understanding of nutrients.

PROTEIN

Protein is essential for building and repairing body cells and tissues, and is particularly important for growing children. No other nutrient can supply the necessary material for growth. Protein is also needed to make antibodies and enzymes.

It is composed of amino acids, some of which are made in the body. Others, known as **essential amino acids**, have to be taken in through food. Animal protein provides all the essential amino acids and is said to be of high biological value (HBV). Vegetable/plant protein, which contains only some of the essential amino acids, has a low biological value (LBV). LBV foods should be eaten in a variety of combinations and mixtures to ensure all the essential amino acids are obtained – this is known as **protein complementation**.

See the chart on page 17 and the diagrams on pages 11, 12 and 13.

FATS

Fats are a concentrated form of energy. They also provide warmth and protect organs such as the heart and kidneys. Food is made more palatable by the addition of fat – think how much more tasty a slice of bread or toast is, if it is spread with butter or margarine rather than eaten dry.

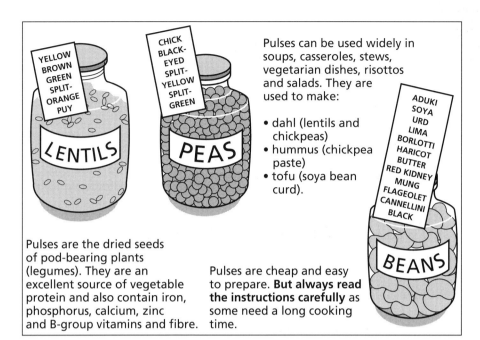

YELLOW
BROWN
GREEN
SPLIT-
ORANGE
PUY

LENTILS

CHICK
BLACK-
EYED
SPLIT-
YELLOW
SPLIT-
GREEN

PEAS

Pulses can be used widely in
soups, casseroles, stews,
vegetarian dishes, risottos
and salads. They are
used to make:

• dahl (lentils and
  chickpeas)
• hummus (chickpea
  paste)
• tofu (soya bean
  curd).

ADUKI
SOYA
URD
LIMA
BORLOTTI
HARICOT
BUTTER
RED KIDNEY
MUNG
FLAGEOLET
CANNELLINI
BLACK

BEANS

Pulses are the dried seeds
of pod-bearing plants
(legumes). They are an
excellent source of vegetable
protein and also contain iron,
phosphorus, calcium, zinc
and B-group vitamins and fibre.

Pulses are cheap and easy
to prepare. **But always read
the instructions carefully** as
some need a long cooking
time.

Pulses

Depending on their chemical composition, fats are either saturated, unsaturated or polyunsaturated. Generally speaking, people eat too much saturated fat, which is high in cholesterol (see below) and carries the risk of health problems. Polyunsaturated fats, which are low in cholesterol and derived mainly from plant sources (but also found in oily fish), are beneficial to health.

While adults may be advised to reduce their total fat intake, children need fat in their diet as a source of energy and for the fat-soluble vitamins A and D which are found mainly in animal fats.

Cholesterol
Cholesterol is an important fat-like substance made naturally in the body and also obtained from animal products, such as egg yolk, fat meat and meat products, butter, cream, dripping and lard, hard cheeses, shrimps and prawns. It is used to make cell membranes and the covering of nerve fibres. It also helps digestion of fats and the production of male and female sex hormones.

Too much saturated fat in the diet raises the level of cholesterol in the body and increases the risk of coronary heart disease and obesity – common health problems in affluent societies where there is a high intake of animal fats. Polyunsaturated fats help to lower the cholesterol level in the body.

See the chart on page 18.

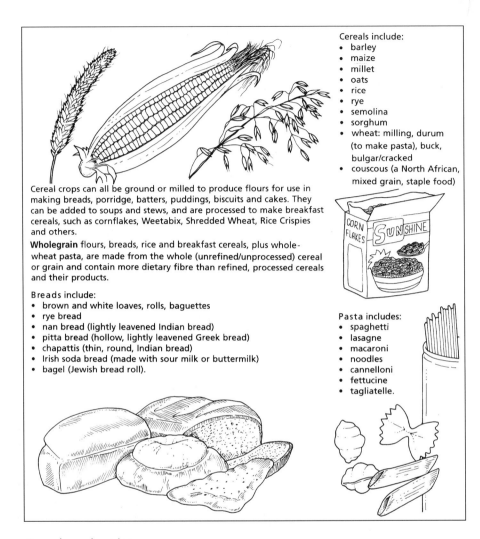

Cereals include:
- barley
- maize
- millet
- oats
- rice
- rye
- semolina
- sorghum
- wheat: milling, durum (to make pasta), buck, bulgar/cracked
- couscous (a North African, mixed grain, staple food)

Cereal crops can all be ground or milled to produce flours for use in making breads, porridge, batters, puddings, biscuits and cakes. They can be added to soups and stews, and are processed to make breakfast cereals, such as cornflakes, Weetabix, Shredded Wheat, Rice Crispies and others.

Wholegrain flours, breads, rice and breakfast cereals, plus whole-wheat pasta, are made from the whole (unrefined/unprocessed) cereal or grain and contain more dietary fibre than refined, processed cereals and their products.

Breads include:
- brown and white loaves, rolls, baguettes
- rye bread
- nan bread (lightly leavened Indian bread)
- pitta bread (hollow, lightly leavened Greek bread)
- chapattis (thin, round, Indian bread)
- Irish soda bread (made with sour milk or buttermilk)
- bagel (Jewish bread roll).

Pasta includes:
- spaghetti
- lasagne
- macaroni
- noodles
- cannelloni
- fettucine
- tagliatelle.

Cereals and grains

CARBOHYDRATES

Carbohydrates are divided into sugars and starches, and provide the body with energy and warmth. They are grouped, according to their chemical composition, into monosaccharides, disaccharides and polysaccharides.

Starchy carbohydrate foods such as breads, cereals, rice, pasta and starchy vegetables (see the diagram on page 13) are not only high-energy foods, they also contain other essential nutrients, such as vitamins, minerals and fibre. They are relatively cheap and filling. Sugars and sugary sweets and drinks (often referred to as single nutrient foods) provide 'empty calories' – which means they provide calories (energy) but no other nutrients. Fibre, also known as 'unavailable carbohydrate' is discussed on page 14.

See the chart on page 19.

VITAMINS

Vitamins are identified by letters, but some also have chemical names. Although they are only needed in small amounts by the body, vitamins are essential for health. Inadequate intake can lead to deficiency disorders, such as scurvy and rickets, and also to poor growth and health.

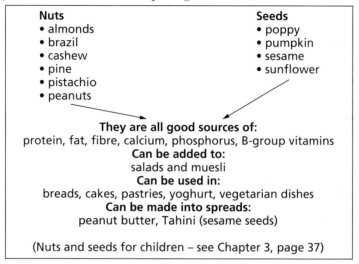

Nuts
- almonds
- brazil
- cashew
- pine
- pistachio
- peanuts

Seeds
- poppy
- pumpkin
- sesame
- sunflower

They are all good sources of:
protein, fat, fibre, calcium, phosphorus, B-group vitamins
Can be added to:
salads and muesli
Can be used in:
breads, cakes, pastries, yoghurt, vegetarian dishes
Can be made into spreads:
peanut butter, Tahini (sesame seeds)

(Nuts and seeds for children – see Chapter 3, page 37)

Nuts and seeds

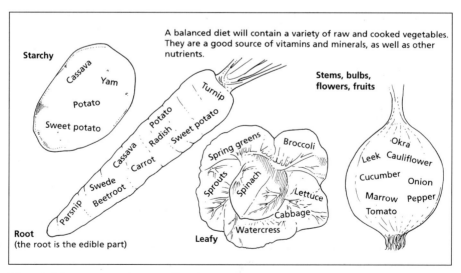

A balanced diet will contain a variety of raw and cooked vegetables. They are a good source of vitamins and minerals, as well as other nutrients.

Starchy
Cassava
Yam
Potato
Sweet potato

Root
(the root is the edible part)
Potato
Cassava
Radish
Sweet potato
Carrot
Swede
Beetroot
Parsnip
Turnip

Leafy
Spring greens
Broccoli
Sprouts
Spinach
Lettuce
Cabbage
Watercress

Stems, bulbs, flowers, fruits
Okra
Leek Cauliflower
Cucumber
Onion
Marrow Pepper
Tomato

Vegetables grouped according to structure

Some vitamins have a specific role in helping the absorption of other essential nutrients. Some, namely A, D, E and K are fat-soluble, which means they can be stored in the body. Others, B-group and C, are water-soluble which means they cannot be stored in the body and are easily destroyed by cooking – foods containing these vitamins need to be eaten daily.

Vitamins, with the exception of D and K, cannot be made in the body and must be taken in through food or vitamin supplements.

See the chart on page 20 and Table 2.1 (pages 24–5).

MINERALS

Like vitamins, minerals are essential for health. They have to be provided by food or supplements. Minerals are classed as major minerals or trace elements according to the amount needed by the body. Of the major minerals iron is important for the formation of haemoglobin in the red blood cells and the transport of oxygen round the body. Lack of iron leads to anaemia. Sodium and potassium are essential for maintaining the fluid balance in the body and calcium and phosphorus are needed for strong bones and teeth. Trace elements are only needed in very small amounts. Fluoride is probably the best known of the trace elements for its role in helping to prevent tooth decay.

See the chart (page 21) and Table 2.2 (pages 26–7).

DIETARY FIBRE

Dietary fibre is a non-starch polysaccharide. It is not digested and absorbed by humans, has no nutrient or calorific value and is referred to as 'unavailable carbohydrate'. However, it is classed as a nutrient in this book and appears on the nutrient diagram in Chapter 1 because of its overall importance in aiding digestion and absorption of food. It encourages chewing and healthy gums and jaws, as well as promoting bowel health and preventing constipation.

See the chart on page 22.

WATER

We cannot live without water. While people can survive for many weeks fasting from solids but taking in fluids, death would occur within a matter of days if water was not available. The kidneys regulate the water balance in the body, and urine output is a good guide to fluid intake and kidney function. Dehydration occurs when there is insufficient water in the body. Some causes of dehydration are outlined in Chapter 3, page 36.

See the chart on page 23.

The food groups

Foods are usually grouped according to the main nutrient they provide. Putting foods into groups makes it easier to plan meals and menus for children.

As a rule, four groups are identified but, because children have different nutritional needs from adults and require moderate amounts of fat in their diet, a fifth group is included here. The food groups are:

1 **Protein** – foods for growth, body building and repair of tissues: meat, liver, kidney, fish (all kinds), poultry, eggs, pulses
2 **Carbohydrates** – energy-giving foods: breads, cereals, rice, pasta, starchy vegetables
3 **Vitamins, minerals, fibre** – for general good health and prevention of specific disorders (see Chapter 8): fruit and vegetables
4 **Calcium** – for healthy bones and teeth: milk and milk foods
5 **Fats and oils** – concentrated high energy-giving foods: butter, margarines and vegetable spreads, cooking oils, oily fish.

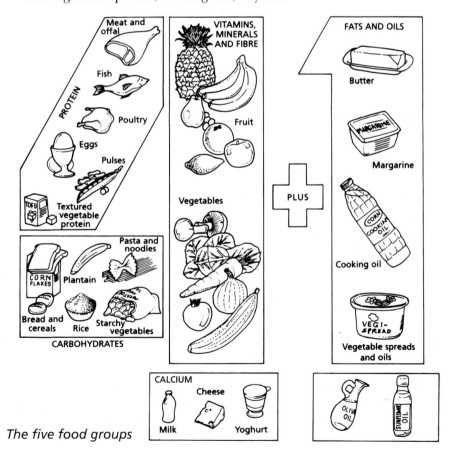

The five food groups

Study the foods in the five groups. Work your way through them and check with your nutrient charts. You will see that there are also other nutrients in each of the foods. For example, meat also contains fat and iron, breads and other starchy foods contain the B–group vitamins and fibre, and milk contains valuable protein, fat and vitamins.

In Chapter 3 you will see how to include foods from these groups in children's diets.

Dairy, staple and fortified foods

DAIRY FOODS

Dairy foods, also known as milk foods, include milk, butter, cheese and yoghurt.

STAPLE FOODS

Staple foods are those which are commonly eaten and form the bulk of a diet. For example, bread and potatoes in Northern Europe, rice in Far-Eastern countries and millet (mealie) in Africa.

FORTIFIED FOODS

Fortified foods are those which have vitamins and/or minerals added to them. Some foods are fortified by law. These are:
- margarine, which has vitamins A and D added
- white flour (and products made from it), which has iron, calcium, vitamin B_1 (Thiamin) and Niacin added.

This helps to ensure that children whose overall diet may be generally poor do not suffer from vitamin or mineral deficiency.

PROTEINS

1 g protein provides 17 kJ/4 kcal

4 TYPES AND SOURCES OF PROTEIN

a Animal

- Meat
- Offal (liver, kidney, heart, tongue, sweetbread)
- Poultry
- Rabbit
- Fish (white and oily)
- Eggs
- Dairy foods

known as 'High Biological Value' (HBV) or **'complete protein'** foods because, by themselves, they supply all the essential amino acids

b Vegetable and plant

- Pulses
- Cereals and cereal-based foods
- Nuts and nut spreads
- Seeds and seed spreads (Pulses and cereals see pages 11 and 12)

known as 'Low Biological Value' (LBV) or **'incomplete protein'** foods because, by themselves, they do not supply all the essential amino acids. A mixture of these foods is needed to provide complete protein. This is known as **protein complementation** (for examples, see Chapter 9 page 126)

5 TEXTURED VEGETABLE PROTEIN (TVP)

- Made mainly from the soya bean
- Nutritive additives (amino acids, B-group vitamins and iron) plus flavouring, colouring and texturing makes it an HBV food resembling beef
- Can be produced in slices, chunks or as mince
- Cheaper than meat
- Acceptable in vegetarian diets

1 COMPOSITION

Made up of amino acids containing carbon, hydrogen, oxygen and nitrogen. The amino nitrogen promotes growth.

Some amino acids are made in the body. Others have to be taken in through food and are known as

ESSENTIAL AMINO ACIDS

Adults need 8 ▼ Children need 10

2 FUNCTIONS

- Provide material for growth and body-building
- Repair and maintain body tissues
- Help to make antibodies and enzymes

3 EFFECTS OF TOO LITTLE

- Poor growth, including brain growth
- Poor healing powers
- Kwashiorkor and marasmus – protein/energy disorders found in poor developing countries

WARNING No other nutrient can be substituted for protein. If carbohydrates and fats do not supply sufficient energy in a child's diet, then protein will be used for energy instead of for its prime function – **growth.**

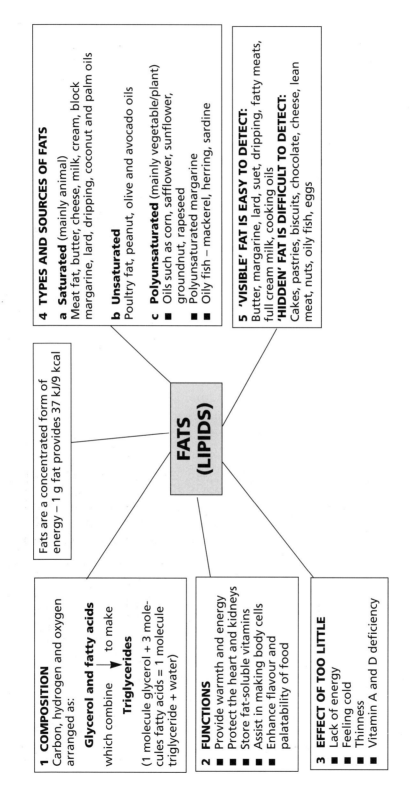

FATS (LIPIDS)

Fats are a concentrated form of energy – 1 g fat provides 37 kJ/9 kcal

1 COMPOSITION
Carbon, hydrogen and oxygen arranged as:

Glycerol and fatty acids which combine → to make **Triglycerides**

(1 molecule glycerol + 3 molecules fatty acids = 1 molecule triglyceride + water)

2 FUNCTIONS
- Provide warmth and energy
- Protect the heart and kidneys
- Store fat-soluble vitamins
- Assist in making body cells
- Enhance flavour and palatability of food

3 EFFECT OF TOO LITTLE
- Lack of energy
- Feeling cold
- Thinness
- Vitamin A and D deficiency

4 TYPES AND SOURCES OF FATS

a Saturated (mainly animal)
Meat fat, butter, cheese, milk, cream, block margarine, lard, dripping, coconut and palm oils

b Unsaturated
Poultry fat, peanut, olive and avocado oils

c Polyunsaturated (mainly vegetable/plant)
- Oils such as corn, safflower, sunflower, groundnut, rapeseed
- Polyunsaturated margarine
- Oily fish – mackerel, herring, sardine

5 'VISIBLE' FAT IS EASY TO DETECT:
Butter, margarine, lard, suet, dripping, fatty meats, full cream milk, cooking oils
'HIDDEN' FAT IS DIFFICULT TO DETECT:
Cakes, pastries, biscuits, chocolate, cheese, lean meat, nuts, oily fish, eggs

REMEMBER
Too much fat in the diet will lead to obesity and other health problems

CARBOHYDRATES

1 COMPOSITION
Compounds of carbon, hydrogen and oxygen divided into: **sugars** and **starches**

2 FUNCTIONS
Provide energy and warmth

3 EFFECTS OF TOO LITTLE
- Lack of energy
- Feeling cold
- Thinness

4
Carbohydrates are the main food group in our diet

5
'Ordinary' sugar (sucrose) is made from sugar cane and sugar beet. It can be:

a Refined – better known as 'table sugar' and also used in the manufacture and processing of many foods

b Unrefined – retains natural molasses and can be used in the same way as refined

Both types are high in joules/calories, are potentially harmful to dental health and can lead to obesity

6 SUGARS

a Monosaccharides (simple sugars)
(formed from one sugar unit)

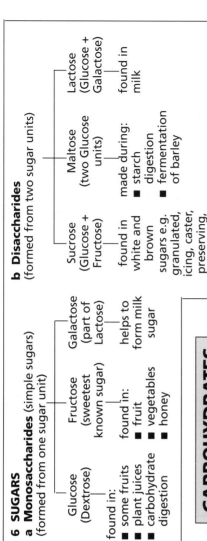

Glucose (Dextrose)
found in:
- some fruits
- plant juices
- carbohydrate digestion

Fructose (sweetest known sugar)
found in:
- fruit
- vegetables
- honey

Galactose (part of Lactose)
helps to form milk sugar

b Disaccharides
(formed from two sugar units)

Sucrose (Glucose + Fructose)
found in white and brown sugars e.g. granulated, icing, caster, preserving, demerara, etc.

Maltose (two Glucose units)
made during:
- starch digestion
- fermentation of barley

Lactose (Glucose + Galactose)
found in milk

c Polysaccharides (complex carbohydrates)
(formed from many sugar units)

Starchy carbohydrate
found in:
- grains/cereals
- starchy vegetables
- plantain (green bananas)
- breadfruit (see page 12)

Non-starch polysaccharides

Fibre (unavailable carbohydrate) (see Chapter 3 pages 35–6)

7 SUGAR IS FOUND IN:
- Fruit, vegetables, honey, milk (occurs naturally (see above))
- Table sugars
- Jams and marmalades (low-sugar preserves available)
- Cakes, pastries, biscuits
- Puddings and jellies
- Tinned fruits (tinned fruit in natural juice is available)
- Sweetened cereals
- Processed foods
- Bottled sauces
- Sweets and chocolates
- A variety of soft drinks

1 g carbohydrate provides 17 kJ/4 kcal

VITAMINS

1
- Vitamins are organic substances found in plants and animals.
- They are present in minute amounts in foods and measured in:
  - micrograms (μg), or
  - milligrams (mg)

2
- Vitamins are needed in very small amounts by the body but **are essential for health**
- Their main function is to assist enzyme activity
- When absent from the diet, deficiency disorders and restricted growth occur

3
- Vitamins cannot be made in the body (except D and K) and must be taken in through food or as supplements
- A balanced, varied diet contains all the vitamins necessary for health

4 VITAMINS CAN BE:
a Fat-soluble → stored in the body

Vitamins A, D, E, K

b Water-soluble → not stored in the body – excess excreted in urine → need to be taken daily

Vitamins B-group and C

Because fat-soluble vitamins are stored in the body, they can accumulate to dangerous levels if too much taken in

5 TO KEEP VITAMIN CONTENT OF FOOD AS HIGH AS POSSIBLE:
- Eat foods as fresh as possible – storage affects vitamin content
- Eat raw fruit and vegetables when possible
- Cut/chop fruit and vegetables just before cooking or eating – exposing cut surfaces to air for long periods reduces vitamin content
- Cook fruit and vegetables quickly in small amount of water. Use cooking liquid to make gravy or sauce
- Steam rather than boil fruit and vegetables

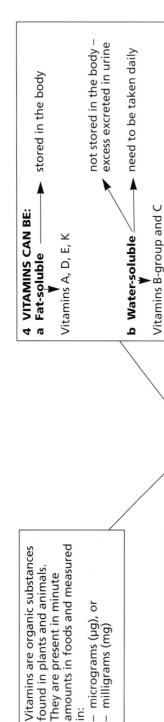

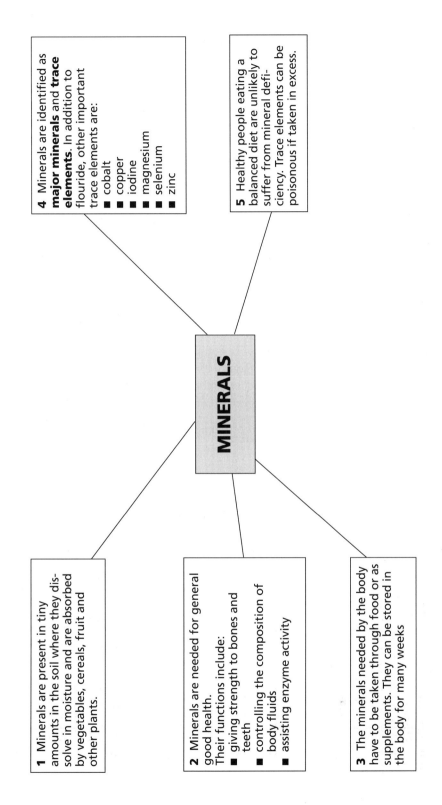

MINERALS

1 Minerals are present in tiny amounts in the soil where they dissolve in moisture and are absorbed by vegetables, cereals, fruit and other plants.

2 Minerals are needed for general good health.
Their functions include:
■ giving strength to bones and teeth
■ controlling the composition of body fluids
■ assisting enzyme activity

3 The minerals needed by the body have to be taken through food or as supplements. They can be stored in the body for many weeks

4 Minerals are identified as **major minerals** and **trace elements**. In addition to flouride, other important trace elements are:
■ cobalt
■ copper
■ iodine
■ magnesium
■ selenium
■ zinc

5 Healthy people eating a balanced diet are unlikely to suffer from mineral deficiency. Trace elements can be poisonous if taken in excess.

THE ESSENTIAL NUTRIENTS **21**

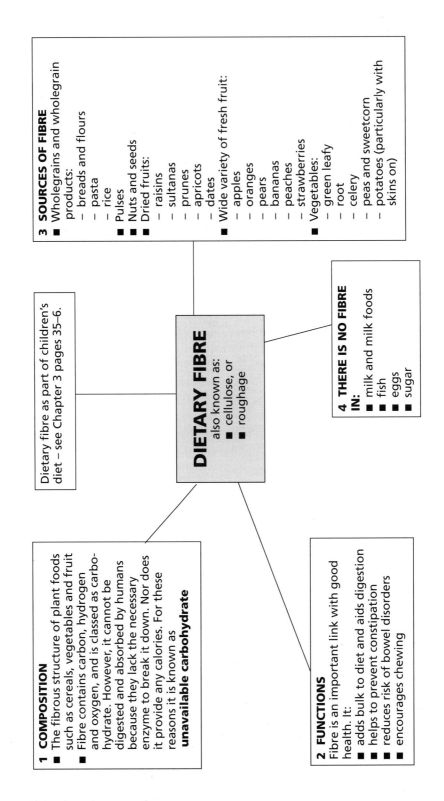

DIETARY FIBRE

also known as:
- cellulose, or
- roughage

Dietary fibre as part of children's diet – see Chapter 3 pages 35–6.

3 SOURCES OF FIBRE
- Wholegrains and wholegrain products:
  - breads and flours
  - pasta
  - rice
- Pulses
- Nuts and seeds
- Dried fruits:
  - raisins
  - sultanas
  - prunes
  - apricots
  - dates
- Wide variety of fresh fruit:
  - apples
  - oranges
  - pears
  - bananas
  - peaches
  - strawberries
- Vegetables:
  - green leafy
  - root
  - celery
  - peas and sweetcorn
  - potatoes (particularly with skins on)

4 THERE IS NO FIBRE IN:
- milk and milk foods
- fish
- eggs
- sugar

1 COMPOSITION
- The fibrous structure of plant foods such as cereals, vegetables and fruit
- Fibre contains carbon, hydrogen and oxygen, and is classed as carbohydrate. However, it cannot be digested and absorbed by humans because they lack the necessary enzyme to break it down. Nor does it provide any calories. For these reasons it is known as **unavailable carbohydrate**

2 FUNCTIONS
Fibre is an important link with good health. It:
- adds bulk to diet and aids digestion
- helps to prevent constipation
- reduces risk of bowel disorders
- encourages chewing

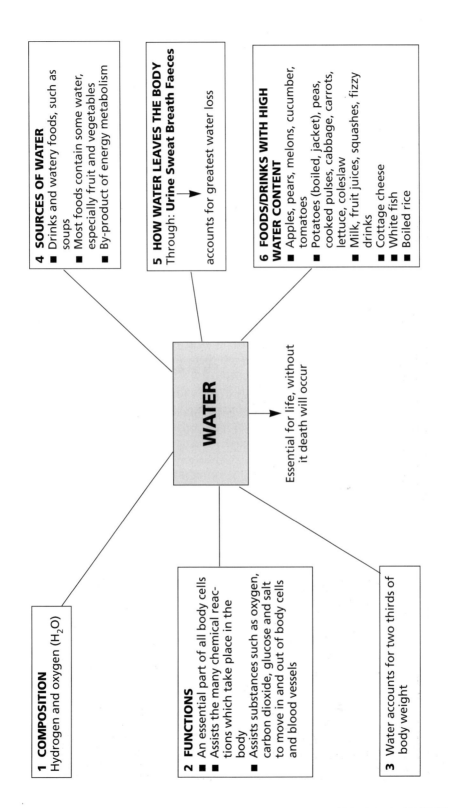

WATER

Essential for life, without it death will occur

1 COMPOSITION
Hydrogen and oxygen (H_2O)

2 FUNCTIONS
- An essential part of all body cells
- Assists the many chemical reactions which take place in the body
- Assists substances such as oxygen, carbon dioxide, glucose and salt to move in and out of body cells and blood vessels

3 Water accounts for two thirds of body weight

4 SOURCES OF WATER
- Drinks and watery foods, such as soups
- Most foods contain some water, especially fruit and vegetables
- By-product of energy metabolism

5 HOW WATER LEAVES THE BODY
Through: **Urine Sweat Breath Faeces**

accounts for greatest water loss

6 FOODS/DRINKS WITH HIGH WATER CONTENT
- Apples, pears, melons, cucumber, tomatoes
- Potatoes (boiled, jacket), peas, cooked pulses, cabbage, carrots, lettuce, coleslaw
- Milk, fruit juices, squashes, fizzy drinks
- Cottage cheese
- White fish
- Boiled rice

Table 2.1 Vitamins

Name of vitamin	Sources	Functions	Effects of too little	Notes
Vitamin A 1 Retinol	■ Animal fats ■ Dairy foods ■ Fortified margarine ■ Eggs ■ Liver ■ Oily fish ■ Fish liver oils	■ Promotes healthy skin, hair, nails, respiratory tract ■ Aids good vision in dim light ■ Promotes growth	■ Poor resistance to infection especially skin and chest ■ Poor night vision ■ Blindness (if extreme deficiency) ■ Delayed growth	■ Fat-soluble ■ Excess vitamin A intake during pregnancy may harm baby. Pregnant women advised not to eat liver because of its high vitamin A content, nor to take vitamin A supplement
2 Carotene (orange/yellow pigment)	■ Green leafy vegetables ■ Carrots ■ Tomatoes ■ Apricots ■ Mangoes ■ Peaches			

B-group
B$_1$ Thiamin
B$_2$ Riboflavin
Niacin
B$_6$ Pyridoxine
B$_{12}$ Cyanocobalamin
	■ Meat
	■ Liver
	■ Milk
	■ Green vegetables
	■ Pulses
	■ Whole grains
	■ Yeast
	■ Eggs
	■ Breakfast cereals
		■ Aids:
		  – healthy working of muscles and nerves
		  – conversion of carbohydrate to energy and iron to haemoglobin
		■ Promotes healthy teeth and gums
		■ Guards against anaemia
			■ Muscle wasting
			■ Digestive problems
			■ Loss of appetite
			■ Anaemia
			■ Deficiency disorders:
			  – Beri beri
			  – Pellagra
			  – Pernicious anaemia
				■ Water-soluble
				■ Tend to occur in same foods
				■ Easily destroyed in cooking
				■ Usually added to breakfast cereals

Folic acid/Folate	■ Liver ■ Potatoes ■ Green leafy vegetables ■ Bread ■ Fortified breakfast cereals	■ Guards against anaemia ■ Helps reduce risk of foetal neural tube defects	Linked to anencephaly and spina bifida in the newborn (failure of brain and spinal cord to develop properly)	■ Easily destroyed in cooking ■ Supplements recommended pre-conceptually and in early pregnancy

(continued)

Table 2.1 Vitamins *continued*

Name of vitamin	Sources	Functions	Effects of too little	Notes

Vitamin C (Ascorbic acid)	■ Citrus fruits
	  – oranges
	  – lemons
	  – limes
	  – grapefruit
	■ Strawberries
	■ Blackcurrants
	■ Pure fruit juices
	■ Sweet peppers
	■ Guavas
	■ Potatoes
	■ Tomatoes
	■ Green leafy vegetables
		■ Promotes:
		  – healthy skin
		  – healing
		■ Aids:
		  – absorption of iron
		  – teeth and bone formation
		■ Builds strong body tissues and blood vessels
			■ Poor resistance to infection
			■ Delayed healing
			■ Anaemia
			■ Scurvy
				■ Water-soluble
				■ Easily destroyed in cooking and keeping food hot
				■ The content of vitamin C in fruit and vegetables varies according to season, freshness and variety

Vitamin D (Calciferol) 'sunshine vitamin'	■ Fish liver oils
	■ Oily fish
	■ Butter
	■ Eggs
	■ Fortified foods
	  – margarine
	  – infant formula
	■ Milk and cheese (small amount)
	■ Sunlight
		Necessary for:
		■ bone and teeth formation
		■ absorption of calcium and phosphorus
			■ Dental caries
			■ Rickets
				■ Fat-soluble
				■ Can be made in the body (synthesised) by action of sunlight on skin

Vitamin E (Tocopherol)	■ Eggs
	■ Soya products
	■ Wheat germ
	■ Vegetable oils
	■ Green vegetables
	■ Nuts and seeds
		■ Aids:
		  – blood clotting
		  – fat metabolism
		  – production of male and female sex hormones
		■ Promotes healing
			■ Heart and blood disorders
			■ Muscle and tissue damage
			■ May contribute to miscarriages
				Fat-soluble, but cannot be stored for long

Vitamin K	■ Green vegetables ■ Alfalfa ■ Soya bean ■ Whole grains ■ Egg yolk ■ Liver	Needed for: ■ clotting of blood ■ wound healing	■ Excessive bleeding ■ Delayed healing	■ Fat-soluble ■ Can be made from bacteria in the intestine ■ Given routinely in some instances to infants at birth

Table 2.2 Minerals

Major minerals	Sources	Functions	Effects of too little	Notes

Iron	■ Meat, liver, kidney
	■ Egg yolk
	■ Oily fish
	■ Green leafy vegetables
	■ Wholemeal bread
	■ Fortified white breads and breakfast cereals
	■ Pulses
	■ Dried fruits
	  – apricots
	  – prunes
	  – raisins and sultanas
	■ Cocoa
		Forms haemoglobin which carries oxygen to all body tissues	Iron-deficiency anaemia:
			■ lack of energy
			■ breathlessness
			■ palor
			■ infections
			■ delayed growth
				■ Vitamin C aids absorption so green vegetables, salads, potatoes, fresh fruit at mealtimes are important
				■ Tannin in tea inhibits iron absorption
				■ Iron especially important:
				  – in childhood and adolescence
				  – during pregnancy and lactation

Calcium	■ Dairy foods
	■ Pulses
	■ Fish and fish bones (sardines, pilchards salmon)
	■ Watercress and other green leafy vegetables
	■ Fortified flours and breads
	■ Hard water
		■ Maintains strong bones and teeth
		■ Aids:
		  – normal muscle function
		  – blood clotting
			■ Dental caries
			■ Rickets (bones fail to harden)
			■ Muscle cramps
			■ Delayed blood clotting
				■ Vitamin D aids absorption
				■ Calcium not well absorbed by body and children unable to eat dairy products should be carefully monitored

Phosphorus	■ Dairy foods ■ Meat ■ Fish ■ Eggs ■ Cereals ■ Fruit and vegetables and most other foods	■ Combines with calcium for strong bones and teeth ■ Aids absorption of carbohydrate ■ Helps to maintain fluid balance in body	Deficiency rare but can occur in kidney disease	High intake in first few days of life from using unmodified cow's milk may result in tetany (muscle spasms)

(continued)

Table 2.2 *Minerals continued*

Major minerals	Sources	Functions	Effects of too little	Notes
Sodium chloride (salt)	■ Common salt ■ Fresh meat and fish ■ Processed foods ■ Cured bacon and ham ■ Smoked fish (kippers) ■ Crisps (salted)	■ Maintains fluid balance in body ■ Aids transmission of nerve impulses ■ Assists muscle activity	■ Muscle cramps ■ Tiredness	■ A high intake of salt is linked to high blood pressure ■ Salt should not be added to foods for babies and young children
Potassium	■ Meat ■ Milk ■ Wholegrain cereals/foods ■ Fruit ■ Vegetables ■ Coffee	Works closely with sodium in maintaining fluid balance	Dietary deficiency rare	■ Widely distributed in fresh foods ■ Coffee unsuitable for young children
Trace elements				
Fluoride	■ Fluoridated water ■ Bones of fish (sardines, pilchards, salmon) ■ Fluoride tablets or drops ■ Toothpaste	Makes tooth enamel more resistant to decay	Dental caries	■ Too much fluoride can cause mottling of teeth and delay shedding ■ Fluoridation of water supplies is a controversial policy

QUICK CHECK

1 Name the seven essential nutrients.
2 How many food groups are there?
3 Name the foods in each of the food groups.
4 Explain the importance in the diet of:
   a) protein
   b) carbohydrate
   c) iron.
5 What do you understand by the terms 'high biological value' protein and 'low biological value' protein?
6 What do you understand by protein complementation?
7 Name the two minerals needed for the formation of bones and teeth.
8 Name the vitamins necessary for the absorption of:
   a) calcium
   b) iron.
9 Describe the terms:
   a) fat-soluble
   b) water-soluble.
10 Name the fat-soluble and water-soluble vitamins.
11 Name the principal nutrients in the following foods:
   a) white fish
   b) red meat
   c) lentils
   d) milk
   e) cheese
   f) wholegrain bread
   g) pasta and rice
   h) potatoes
   i) carrots
   j) broccoli
   k) tomatoes
   l) oranges
   m) strawberries
   n) cream
   o) butter
   p) fortified margarine
   q) peanuts.
12 Which foods are known as 'dairy foods'?
13 Name the staple foods of Northern Europe and Africa.
14 What do you understand by the term 'fortified foods'?
15 Why are some foods fortified?

KEY WORDS AND TERMS

You need to know what these words and phrases mean. Go back through the chapter and find out.

amino acids
animal protein
vegetable protein
high and low biological value
protein complementation
saturated and polyunsaturated fat

unavailable carbohydrate
food groups
dairy foods
staple foods
fortified foods

3 BALANCED DIETS

> **This chapter covers:**
> - A well-balanced diet
> - The principles of feeding children
> - Daily portion intakes
> - Healthy snacks
> - Planning balanced menus
> - Dietary needs in adolescence, preconceptually and in pregnancy

Common health problems among the adult population in the UK include:
- obesity
- dental disease
- high blood pressure
- coronary heart disease
- arthritis
- diabetes (late onset)
- varicose veins
- constipation
- haemorrhoids
- large bowel disorders.

While changing lifestyles, smoking and lack of exercise may contribute to some of these problems, incorrect or poor diet is a major factor. Even very young children suffer from obesity, dental disease and constipation. Carers and professional child care workers have a responsibility to provide healthy, nutritious food for children and help them to establish good eating patterns and healthy attitudes to food, which will reduce the risk of dietary disorders both in childhood and adult life.

During the first year of life physical growth is rapid. Growth then continues at a slower, steadier rate. With adolescence comes a further period of rapid growth. Appetite is influenced by growth rate and so infants and adolescents will want more food. Growing children require more nutrients, in relation to their size, than adults. Their diet must be balanced and contain a wide variety of foods from all the food groups. On the whole, children eat too much fat, sugar, salt and additives, and insufficient wholegrains, fruit and vegetables.

Any changes to children's diets should be made slowly. Try setting an example by eating and enjoying healthy food yourself. Introducing children to a wide range of foods early on and involving them in menu planning, buying and preparing food will promote an interest in what they are eating and increase their knowledge of different foods and where they come from.

Good nutrition and dietary principles in infancy should lead to correct eating habits in the future. It is essential that carers understand what constitutes a balanced diet and the principles involved in feeding young children.

A well-balanced diet

A well-balanced diet is one in which a **wide variety** of foods from the food groups is eaten daily. This means there will be no great excess or deficiency of a nutrient. If a particular nutrient is not in one food, it will be in another. A varied diet, which may include foods from different cultures, will provide children with the nutrients they need for growth and good health. It will also offer them a wide choice in what they eat. Children need three meals and two or three healthy snacks a day.

Dinner time in the nursery

You can check whether a child's diet is adequate by assessing her:
- state of health
- growth and development pattern

■ energy output.

Any assessment of the nutrient content of a child's diet should be carried out over a period of two to three weeks and not made on one day's dietary intake.

The chart below outlines how a balanced diet promotes health and development in children.

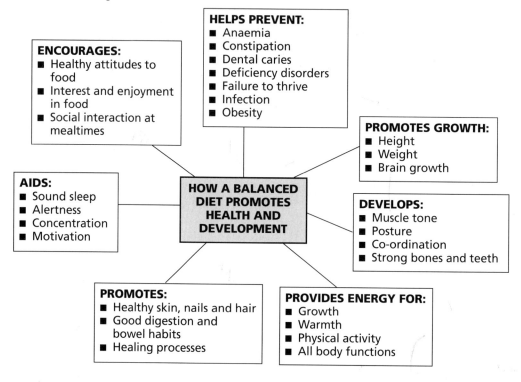

The principles of feeding children

PROTEIN AND ENERGY

The first nutritional requirements for children are for protein and energy.

Protein

The need for protein is great during the periods of rapid growth in infancy and adolescence, and also during the steady growth in childhood years. It is also needed at times of injury and infection.

Too little protein in early life, when the brain is developing rapidly, may result in learning delay as well as poor weight and height growth. Children may, for reasons of culture, religion or parental preference, be offered vegetable rather than animal sources of protein, so a **wide variety and mixture** of pulses and cereal foods will be needed to ensure they receive all the amino acids necessary for growth.

Using up energy in the playground

Energy

Children need energy for growth and to replace energy used up in their busy, active day. Their calorie requirement is high and should be supplied by:

- carbohydrate foods such as breads, cereals, pasta and rice, plus starchy vegetables (see Chapter 2, pages 12–13, 19)
- fats and oils. While low-fat diets may be recommended for adults, they are very unsuitable for children. Fats and oils are an important source of energy for young children. They are, however, a much more concentrated form of energy than carbohydrates, providing twice the number of calories per gram. Sensible dietary practice is to cut down, not eliminate, children's intake of saturated fat. Offer lean meat, poultry and polyunsaturated sources of fat such as oily fish (sardines, mackerel and herring) and corn, sunflower, soya spreads and oils. Animal fats provide important fatty acids and fat-soluble vitamins. Fried foods, such as chips, and foods with a high fat content, such as cream, biscuits, cakes, pastry, crisps, chocolate, can be offered occasionally.

REMEMBER!

There is no substitute for protein. If energy requirements are not met by carbohydrates and fats, protein will be used instead to supply essential energy rather than being used to promote growth.

MILK

Whole (full-fat) milk is one of the most complete foods available and plays an important part in a healthy diet for children, especially those whose diet may be generally poor. It is a rich source of protein and fat, calcium and phosphorus, vitamin A and the B-group vitamins. It also contains some vitamin C and D. The content of vitamins A, B_2 (Riboflavin) and C are reduced if the milk is exposed to sunlight, for example when it is left on a doorstep for some time.

The Department of Health recommends 1 pint of whole milk daily for children under 5 years, especially for its fat (energy) content and vitamins A and D. Carers who wish to give a child over 2 years semi-skimmed milk may do so, but they should check that the overall diet is balanced and wholesome with other foods providing necessary energy and fat-soluble vitamins. Skimmed milk is not suitable for children under 5 years as it limits their intake of fat and so affects their calorie and fat-soluble vitamin intake. Children may be offered milk in a variety of ways – as a drink, in puddings, custard and sauces, with cereals or as cheese or plain yoghurt.

The energy, protein and fat content of milks
- One pint whole milk provides:
  1610 kJ/387 kcal
  19 g protein
  23 g fat
- One pint semi-skimmed milk provides:
  1145 kJ/270 kcal
  19.4 g protein
  9.4 g fat
- One pint of skimmed milk provides:
  824 kJ/194 kcal
  19.4 g protein
  0.6 g fat

REMEMBER!

Whole, semi-skimmed and skimmed milks are all good sources of calcium and phosphorus.

Bottled milk can be identified by the colour of the bottle top:
- pasteurised whole milk – silver top
- pasteurised semi-skimmed milk – red/white top
- pasteurised skimmed milk – blue/white top
- Channel Islands milk (high fat content) – gold top
- untreated milk – green top
- sterilised milk – long-necked glass bottle with a crown cap.

SUGAR

Sugar provides nothing but 'empty' calories. It is not necessary as a source of energy – starchy carbohydrates and other nutrients will provide all the energy a child needs. Many foods such as milk, fruit and vegetables contain natural sugar, but these foods also provide other essential nutrients such as vitamins, minerals and fibre.

On the whole, natural sugars make up only a small proportion of the total sugar eaten. It is the refined sugars **added** to foods and drinks that constitute a threat to health. These include white and brown table sugars which provide about 20 kcal per teaspoon.

Sugar should not be added to children's food and drinks. Foods such as cakes and pastries, biscuits, jam, sweets, chocolates and sugary drinks lead to dental caries (decay) and obesity. These foods cannot be totally excluded from children's diets but try to reduce them to a minimum. Processed foods, such as baked beans, bottled sauces, salad dressings and jams, usually contain sugar. Check labels of such foods for sugar, dextrose or glucose content (for more about labelling, see Chapter 7). Pure fruit juice or fresh or dried fruits can be used as cereal and pudding sweeteners if necessary. Low-sugar/sugar-free jams are available. Jelly can be home-made using unsweetened fruit juice. Sweet flavoured vegetables such as carrots, celery and sweet corn are appetising.

SALT

High salt (sodium chloride) intake in childhood is linked to high blood pressure in later life. In turn, raised blood pressure increases the risk of coronary heart disease, stroke and kidney disease.

The immature kidneys of an infant are unable to cope with salt, but after 1 year there is less risk of kidney damage. However, salt is not needed when preparing and cooking food for children and the use of table salt should be discouraged. The amount of salt occurring naturally in many foods is sufficient for the body's needs and it is better for children's health if they do not develop a taste for salty foods. Fresh herbs will enhance the flavour of foods if necessary. As with sugar, most processed foods contain salt. Read the labels of these foods looking for words such as salt, soy or sodium (glutamate, bicarbonate, nitrate or nitrite). (See Chapter 7.)

FIBRE

A high-fibre diet is unsuitable for children as it fills them up, leaving little room for essential nutrients and it may cause stomach pains. Fibre in the form of raw bran can prevent the absorption of important minerals such as calcium and zinc and should not be given to children.

Offering children wholegrain cereals, bread, pasta and rice (including brown rice pudding), as well as fruit (fresh and dried), assorted raw and cooked vegetables and jacket potatoes will provide them with adequate fibre. Pulses are a good source of fibre and can be used in casseroles, soups, flans, salads and burgers. Red kidney beans are used in chilli con carne, and dahl is made from lentils and chick peas. Wholemeal flour can be used for baking. All these foods will encourage chewing, promote healthy bowel habits and reduce the risk of constipation.

WATER AND OTHER DRINKS

Water and milk with occasional drinks of diluted, unsweetened fruit juice should provide the fluid intake for children. Offer them regular drinks of water at and between mealtimes, especially in hot weather or whenever they are thirsty. Babies under 1 year can have cooled boiled water. Tea and coffee are not advised as drinks for young children. They both contain the stimulant caffeine. Tannin, found in tea, inhibits the absorption of iron and, of course, sugar added to tea or coffee can affect dental health and contribute to overweight.

The minerals sodium (salt) and potassium, together with the kidneys, play a vital role in maintaining the fluid balance in the body – too much or too little of either mineral can affect health, as can a variety of kidney disorders. Natural mineral waters are unsuitable for young children as the sodium content may overload their kidneys, and if the fluoride level is high, there is danger of damage to tooth enamel.

Providing children with a sensible range of food and adequate drinks will keep their sodium, potassium and water levels in balance and prevent thirst.

REMEMBER!

Dehydration (loss of water from the body) can be caused by:
- diarrhoea and vomiting
- high temperature
- mouth and throat infections which make drinking and swallowing painful
- diabetes
- insufficient fluid intake during hot weather.

These conditions can be serious and you should always seek advice if you are concerned about a baby or young child.

FRUIT AND VEGETABLES

Fruit and vegetables are excellent sources of vitamins, minerals and fibre and many have a high water content. Cooking and processing destroys much of the vitamin content, so remember to offer children raw sticks of vegetables as well as a variety of fresh and dried fruits.

NUTS AND SEEDS

Whole or broken nuts and large seeds are unsuitable for young children under 4 years because of the danger of choking. Ground nuts and seeds can be used in baking, cooking or spreads. Tahini and peanut butter spreads make nutritious fillings for sandwiches.

Peanut allergy is always a possibility so check with the carers before giving peanut butter to a child in the nursery. A severe reaction to peanuts can include swelling of the face and neck leading to constriction of the airways, breathing difficulties and the danger of suffocation. Allergies and intolerances are discussed in Chapter 6, pages 84–7.

DIETARY SUPPLEMENTS

Daily supplements of vitamins A, D and C, available from the Child Health Clinic, are recommended for children under 5 years.

REMEMBER!

- Children need a high protein and high energy diet.
- Whole milk is advisable up to 2 years and preferably up to 5 years.
- Offer foods that are low in salt and sugar. No added salt or sugar.
- Provide fibre in the form of wholegrains, fruit (fresh and dried) and raw and cooked vegetables. No raw bran.

Should these be on the nursery or school meal table?

- Adequate fluid, especially water, is necessary.
- No whole or broken nuts and seeds under 4 years (don't forget peanut allergy).
- Vitamin supplements up to 5 years.

Daily portion intakes

Recommended daily portion intakes for children are:
- two portions of meat or other protein foods, such as pulses or nuts
- two portions of protein from dairy foods (milk, cheese, yoghurt)
- four portions of cereal foods
- four to five portions of fruit and vegetables
- approximately $1\frac{1}{2}$ pints (1 litre) of fluids, of which 1 pint will be milk.

SOME TYPICAL AVERAGE PORTION SIZES

- Bread, 1 medium slice or $\frac{1}{2}$ large slice   28 g/1 oz
- Cereals: cornflakes, rice crispies, etc.   28–56 g/1–2 oz (3–5 tbsp)
- Weetabix, 1 biscuit   21 g/3–4 oz
- Egg, 1 medium   42 g/$1\frac{1}{2}$ oz
- Meat and poultry   28–56 g/1–2 oz
- Bacon, 1 slice   28 g/1 oz
- Sausage, 1 medium   28 g/1 oz
- Rice (uncooked), 1 tablespoon   28 g/1 oz
- Hard cheese   56 g/2 oz
- Apple, 1 medium   112 g/4 oz
- Carrot, 1 medium   112 g/4 oz
- Potato, 1 medium   112g/4 oz

Children's appetites and nutritional needs vary according to their age, size, gender and energy levels. Many 2–3-year-olds are unpredictable in their eating patterns, eating little one day and everything the next. Some 7–8-year-olds have big appetites eating almost adult-sized meals.

> **Activity**
> Look at Table 3.1 opposite. It shows the nutritional value (per 100 g/$3\frac{1}{2}$ oz) of some commonly eaten foods.
> Copy the table and complete it using information on nutritional labels. Add to it as you learn about and research foods to help you in your understanding and planning of children's meals and snacks.

Table 3.1   The nutritional value of foods, per 100 g ($3\frac{1}{2}$ oz)

Food	Energy kJ	kcal	Protein g	Fat g	Calcium mg	Iron mg	Vitamin A µg	Vitamin C µg
Cheddar cheese	1708	412	26	34	720	0.3	363	0
Cottage cheese	413	98	13.6	4	73	0.1	46	0
Bread (white)	1002	235	8.4	2	110	1.6	0	0
Bread (wholemeal)	914	215	9.2	2.5	54	2.7	0	0
Apple	196	46	0.3	0	4	0.3	5	5
Orange	150	35	0.8	0	41	0.3	8	50
Weetabix								
Baked beans								
Chocolate biscuits								
Butter								
Plain yoghurt								
Rice								

Healthy snacks

Children need two to three healthy snacks a day. They are important in the overall dietary provision for young children, complementing main meals. Snack foods can be interesting, imaginative and colourful and should reflect different cultural tastes. Some examples are:

- pieces of fresh or dried fruits (Dried fruits such as apricots, apples, stoned dates and prunes, pineapple and figs as well as sultanas, currants and raisins are good sources of minerals and fibre.)
- diluted unsweetened pure fruit juice or a milk drink and plain biscuit
- sandwiches using assorted breads and rolls (including wholegrain) with fillings, such as cottage or hard cheese, chicken, ham, tuna fish, yeast extract, peanut butter, salad ingredients, tahini, hummus or banana
- washed raw vegetables, such as carrots, celery and white cabbage cut into managable pieces
- plain yoghurt flavoured with chopped fresh fruit
- milk shake (whole milk flavoured with liquidised fresh fruit).

SAFE PRACTICE

- Use ground rather than whole nuts for children under 4 years.
- Check with carers for peanut allergy.
- Supervision of young children is particularly important when they are eating hard foods, such as carrot and celery sticks and pieces of hard fruit, as choking may occur.
- Remove stones from fruits such as peaches, nectarines and plums. Check for pips in oranges, satsumas and other such fruits.
- Children should sit down to eat meals and snacks. Walking or running around while eating or drinking can contribute to accidents including choking.

Occasional foods

Occasional foods are often called 'junk food'. Processed pies, bought burgers and chips, crisps, cakes and pastries, assorted sweet and chocolate biscuits, powdered desserts and milk drinks, fruit squashes and fizzy drinks, sweets and chocolate are all firm favourites with many children and, in fact, form the basis of many children's diets. They usually contain a lot of fat, salt, sugar and additives, and can be low in vitamins and minerals. They should be offered only **occasionally**.

OFFER REGULARLY

Washed, raw vegetables:
- sticks of carrot and celery
- chunks of cabbage
- pieces of cucumber

Fresh fruit:
- apples
- oranges
- pears
- bananas
- kiwi fruit
- mandarins, etc.

Sandwiches/rolls
(white and wholegrain):
- ham
- hard and cottage cheese
- yeast extract
- salad ingredients
- banana
- peanut butter
- tahini spread

Milk or water to drink

Plain yoghurt

Dried fruits:
- apple rings
- apricots
- figs
- stoned prunes and dates

S

N

A

C

K

S

Chips

Crisps

Chocolate and other sweet biscuits

Fizzy orange drinks

Cola drinks

Bought pies and sausage rolls

Sweets and chocolate bars

Powdered desserts

Powdered milk shakes

Lemonade

Health dangers include dental caries, obesity, vitamin and mineral deficiencies, with the risk of further problems in adult life. Home-made pies and burgers made with lean meat can be very nutritious. To make chips at home, cut potatoes into thick slices (they will soak up less fat), fry in polyunsaturated oil and drain on kitchen paper. Low fat and salt-free crisps are available.

Planning balanced menus

When planning menus for children you need to consider which foods will supply the essential nutrients, how much food they need and what religious, cultural or other dietary needs they have. This will mean talking to parents/carers and finding out about dietary habits and likes and dislikes. You now have the theory for planning children's meals and snacks with five sources of knowledge to help you:
- Dietary Reference Values (Chapter 1)
- essential nutrients and food groups (Chapter 2)
- principles of feeding children (Chapter 3)
- daily portion requirements (Chapter 3)
- snacks – their importance and examples (Chapter 3).

Activity
Would you change any of the following meals or snacks for children? Give reasons for both 'yes' and 'no' answers.
a) Cornflakes, skimmed milk and sugar, drink of sweet tea.
b) Fried bacon, sausage and chips, baked beans, tomato sauce, white bread and butter, drink of milk.
c) Home-made cheese and onion flan, baked potato, green salad and tomatoes, followed by fresh fruit salad and drink of water.
d) Wholewheat cracker spread lightly with butter, cheddar cheese and drink of milk.
e) Bought white burger bun filled with fried beef burger and onions followed by a sticky bun, packet of crisps and can of Cola.
f) Chicken curry, brown rice and poppadom followed by jelly and ice cream, drink of water.
g) Warm chocolate drink and plain biscuit.
h) Bought meat pie, tinned carrots, mashed potatoes followed by tinned rice pudding and jam, fizzy orange drink.
i) Home-made cottage pie and peas, followed by stewed apples and custard, drink of water.
j) Baked white fish (boned), broccoli and mashed potatoes with

parsley sauce, followed by a piece of fresh fruit and drink of milk.

k) Spaghetti bolognese followed by syrup sponge pudding and chocolate sauce, can of Cola.

l) Breakfast cereal and chopped dried fruit with milk, grilled sausage and slice of wholemeal bread, diluted unsweetened fruit juice to drink.

m) Lentil and chickpea casserole, wholegrain rice and mixed frozen vegetables, followed by plain yoghurt with chopped fresh fruit and drink of water.

n) Drink of milk, packet of cheese and onion crisps and two custard cream biscuits.

o) Bowl of home-made vegetable soup, wholemeal roll and butter, fresh apple and milky unsweetened tea to drink.

Dietary needs in adolescence, preconceptually and in pregnancy

ADOLESCENCE

Adolescence is a time of rapid growth. It is also a time when young people take more control over their lives including what they eat. Meals may be missed due to pressures of school or college work. Living and working away from home may mean irregular eating patterns and poor nutrient intake. Adolescents are greatly influenced by their peers and may wish to eat vegetarian foods to be like their best friend or out of concern and respect for animals. They may be sensitive or embarrassed about their weight or acne and adopt a strict dietary regime. Some, mainly girls, may develop anorexia.

Adolescents need to know what constitutes a healthy, balanced diet whether or not they are living at home and whether they eat meat or are vegetarians. Snacks may be an important part of their overall nutrient intake. They need approximately 2000–3000 kilocalories daily (boys needing more than girls) and should be encouraged to eat foods high in starchy carbohydrates rather than fatty foods. Fresh fruit and vegetables and whole grains should be eaten to provide vitamins, minerals and fibre.

PRECONCEPTION

A balanced diet preconceptually (before conception) allows a woman to store essential nutrients in her body in readiness for her planned baby. Dieting to lose weight is inadvisable as important nutrients may be missed out.

Especially important is folic acid (folate) which is needed to make foetal cells and for the development of the brain and spinal cord. The brain and spinal cord form early in foetal life and insufficient folic acid may lead to the baby being born with anencephaly or spina bifida. Women need to be advised of foods rich in folic acid and take folic acid supplements preconceptually and during the first 12 weeks of pregnancy. A woman who has previously given birth to a baby with anencephaly or spina bifida will be prescribed folic acid supplements preconceptually by her family doctor.

A balanced diet – healthy mother, healthy babies

The basic principles of healthy eating preconceptually are:
- Eat daily from food groups 1 to 4 (see page 15).
- Eat fresh foods whenever possible.
- Reduce intake of sugar and sugary foods to a mimimum.
- Cut down on fatty foods – eat polyunsaturates rather than saturated fats.
- Cut down on salty foods – a high intake of salt is linked to high blood pressure which can cause problems in pregnancy.

PREGNANCY

During pregnancy a healthy eating pattern is necessary to meet the mother's health needs, prepare her for labour and breast-feeding and also provide for the growth and nourishment of her developing baby. The growing foetus will take whatever nutrients it needs from the mother. Unless her diet is adequate, balanced and nutritious her own health may be affected. If her diet is seriously deficient then both mother and foetus will suffer.

Extra calories are needed for:
- growth of the foetus and foetal structures such as the placenta (after-birth) and amniotic fluid ('waters')
- growth of breast and uterine tissue
- stored energy ready for labour and breast-feeding.

The calories will come partly from diet and partly from naturally conserved energy as a mother rests more during her pregnancy.

The basic principles of healthy eating in pregnancy include:

- Drink an extra pint of milk daily, or eat yoghurt or cheese, to provide calcium for the baby's bones and teeth.
- Eat foods containing iron to guard against anaemia and a possible heavy blood loss during birth. The diet must also meet the foetal need to store iron in the liver.
- Ensure an intake of folic acid-rich foods.
- Eat fresh fruit and vegetables, whole grain breads, pasta and rice to provide fibre which is necessary for good health and to prevent constipation (a common disorder in pregnancy). Bran-enriched cereals and drinks of water will also help.
- Avoid soft cheeses and paté, raw or lightly cooked eggs, and raw or undercooked meat. These carry the risk of infections such as listeria, salmonella and toxoplasmosis respectively, which are harmful to the unborn baby. Liver is not recommended because of its high vitamin A content which may be linked to foetal abnormality.
- Take vitamins, iron and folic acid supplements as advised by the doctor. These are especially important for women on low incomes or income support or who are eating restrictive diets

Women eating vegetarian or vegan diets should follow the principles in Chapter 9 to ensure a balanced, nutritious diet preconceptually and antenatally. Dietary advice is always available from GPs, dieticians, midwives or health visitors.

Activity

Make up a three-day menu of three meals a day for the following expectant mothers:

a) an Asian mother

b) a mother who eats a vegan diet.

QUICK CHECK

1 What are the first nutritional requirements when planning meals for children?
2 What do you understand by the phrase 'a well-balanced diet'?
3 How does a well-balanced diet promote the overall development of children?
4 Name the main nutrients in whole milk. Which of them are affected by exposure to sunlight?
5 Why is skimmed milk unsuitable for young children?

6 Which words on a nutritional label would alert you to the presence in that food of:
   a) sugar?
   b) salt?
7 The use of refined sugars in children's diets contributes to dental caries and obesity. What could you use as a substitute, if necessary, for sweetening foods such as breakfast cereals and puddings?
8 What are the dangers of added salt in the diets of babies and young children?
9 Why are high-fibre diets unsuitable for children?
10 Name some possible causes of dehydration in young children.
11 What factors might influence the choice of food in adolescence?
12 The lack of which vitamin is thought to be linked to spina bifida in the newborn?
13 Why are extra calories needed in pregnancy?
14 What is the importance of iron in the diet of an expectant mother?
15 Why is liver not recommended in the diet during pregnancy?

KEY WORDS AND TERMS

You need to know what these words and phrases mean. Go back through the chapter and find out.

well-balanced diet
protein and energy needs
whole milk nutrient value
empty calories
dehydration

peanut allergy
portion requirements
typical portion sizes
diet preconceptually and in pregnancy

---

4 FEEDING INFANTS

> **This chapter covers:**
> - Breast or bottle?
> - Breast feeding
> - Bottle feeding
> - Weaning
> - Possible feeding difficulties

Breast or bottle?

The choice between bottle- and breast-feeding is an important one for any would-be parent. It is a decision best made after careful consideration of all the health promotion information available. It is a decision for the parents, and not one for carers and health professionals to make and pressure should not be put on the parents to make any particular decision. Such pressure may result in a mother feeling guilty, for example, because she had decided not to breast-feed. This guilt may affect some of the pleasure of the early days of parenthood.

The antenatal period is the ideal time to give information about different feeding methods, as both parents have time to consider all the facts. Research tells us that parents, are especially responsive to health information at this time. Social factors will affect their choice, just as much as health factors.

> **Activities**
> 1 What might influence parents' decisions between breast- and bottle-feeding when considering lifestyle and finance:
>   a) Which is cheaper?
>   b) How much equipment will be needed for each method?
>   c) What is the cost of a packet of formula milk?
>   d) How many packets will be required for one year?
>   e) How many feeding bottles will be required?
>   f) What types and amounts of sterilising equipment will be required?

Breast-feeding

Breast-feeding is nature's 'designer food'. The milk is specific to each individual baby and, although much can be copied in formula milks, the most important parts cannot. It changes as the baby grows and her needs alter.

The rate of a baby's growth is greatest in the first year of life, but especially in the first months – the baby will usually double her birth weight by 5 to 6 months and treble it by 12 months. The largest area of growth in these months is the brain. It is, therefore, very important that a baby's nutritional needs are met fully to allow this important development take place

Breast milk is a complete food for the first months of life and no supplements of other nutrients are required.

HOW BREAST MILK IS MADE

The mature breast varies a great deal in size from one woman to another. The size of breast, nipple and areola (the dark area surrounding the nipple) are not related to the ability to produce milk successfully.

The important aspect of the nipple is its ability to become erect to allow the baby to attach herself to (or 'fix' at) the breast. The milk does not leave the breast through a single channel at the nipple, but through the lactiferous (milk-producing) ducts leading from each of the lobes (see the diagram opposite). (There are 15 to 20 ducts depending on the number of lobes or segments.) The areola also contains a number of small glands called Montgomery's tubercles which become larger and more noticeable during pregnancy. They act like sweat glands and secrete a fluid which helps to keep the nipple soft and supple – a natural moisturing cream that should not be removed by washing with soap.

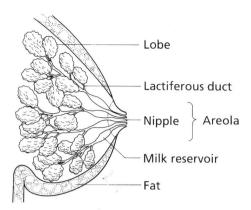

The lactating breast

HOW THE MILK IS RELEASED

Breast milk is released by the 'let-down' reflex (see the diagram below). Some women find this let-down sensation very strong, while others hardly notice it.

The breasts will only produce more milk when existing milk has been removed. Successful breast-feeding depends on 'supply and demand' – the more the baby feeds, the more milk is made. If this mechanism is broken, for example by giving the baby 'extra' in a bottle, future underproduction will result.

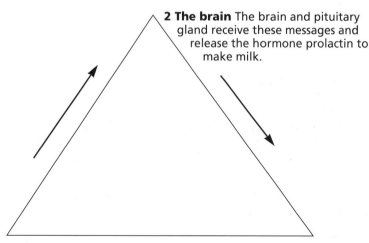

2 The brain The brain and pituitary gland receive these messages and release the hormone prolactin to make milk.

1 The baby The baby sucking at the nipple stimulates the nerve endings in the breast to send messages to the brain.

3 Breast milk The contraction of the muscle comes from the action of the hormone oxytocin, which propels the milk down the ducts to the nipple and into the baby's mouth.

The let-down reflex

THE COMPOSITION OF BREAST MILK

Breast milk is a changing food – it adapts to meet the needs of the growing baby.

Colostrum

This syrupy, yellowish substance is the important first milk made by the breasts from about the fifth month of pregnancy until about ten days after birth.

It protects the newborn baby from her more exposed and potentially dangerous environment outside the womb. It has a much higher protein content than later, mature breast milk and is low in fat and sugar. This is thought to be because:

- The proteins contain many antibodies which line the baby's intestines and prevent harmful bacteria entering the blood stream.
- The high protein levels ensure that even the small amounts taken in will supply sufficient energy to allow the baby to sleep for long periods in the first days after birth.

For these reasons, even when not intending to continue, mothers are often actively encouraged to breast-feed for the first few days.

REMEMBER!

There is no artificial replacement for colostrum.

Mature breast milk

When milk begins to be made in the breasts and 'comes in' on the second to fourth day, it is still mixed with colostrum and looks rich and creamy. By the tenth day the mature milk looks thin and watery by comparison. The change in appearance does not reflect a change in composition, which is natural and appropriate to the baby's needs.

By the end of the fourth week, breast milk contains approximately a fifth of the protein of colostrum and more fat and glucose. The milk at the beginning of a feed is called the 'fore milk'. It is high in lactose (milk sugar) for a quick energy boost. With the let-down reflex comes the 'hind milk' which has a higher fat content and so is rich in calories to meet the baby's growth needs. It also satisfies her for longer.

Human milk is almost completely digestible. The proteins are broken down into soft curds and quickly pass through into the small intestine. Water forms the liquid part of the milk.

All milks are poor sources of iron and babies depend on the stores laid down in their livers during pregnancy. These supplies will last until the baby is 4 to 6 months old. The high concentration of lactose and vitamin C in breast milk help in the absorption of iron.

MANAGEMENT OF BREAST-FEEDING

A mother breast-feeding her baby will benefit from the support you can give her by explaining and answering her questions. She will be helped by understanding that it may take time for her and her baby to get to know each other and that, although breast-feeding is natural, many first-time mothers need additional support to establish feeding patterns.

It is thought to be important for the baby to be put to the breast as soon as possible after birth. This 'skin-to-skin' contact helps the mother and her baby to develop a loving relationship and, in addition, the sucking helps release hormones which contract the uterus.

The mother needs a comfortable position when feeding, for example, she may prefer to lie on her side if her perineum is sore. Pain can reduce the let-down reflex and the flow of milk, so feeding in comfort is important. Chairs should give good support to the lower back, feet can be put on a stool if needed, and privacy provided.

'Fixing' at the breast

The baby will use her rooting reflex to search for the breast. This can best be achieved by stimulating the baby's mouth with the mother's nipple. The baby will then turn to the breast and suck. Take the baby to the breast and never force the breast into the baby's mouth.

The baby is correctly fixed at the breast when she has the nipple and areola in her mouth. Sucking on the nipple alone will cause soreness. When successfully fixed, the baby's mouth will be wide open with the bottom lip curled back and some way from the base of the nipple (see the diagram on page 52). If the baby's nose is pressing into the breast and causing her to come off frequently, she can be helped by repositioning so that her head tilts slightly backwards. Pressing the breast to allow the baby to breathe alters the shape of the nipple and should be avoided.

Breast feeding should not hurt. The mother will feel comfortable when the baby is fixed correctly. This will tell her that her baby is feeding in the right position.

Taking the baby off the breast

The baby should be allowed to come off the breast by herself, when she has

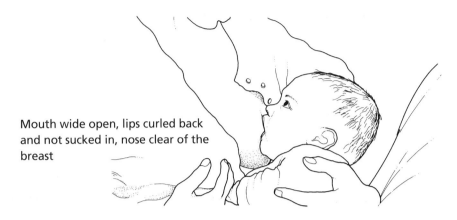

Mouth wide open, lips curled back and not sucked in, nose clear of the breast

The baby fixed correctly at the breast

finished her feed. If she is not fixed correctly, however, the mother can put her finger into the corner of the baby's mouth to release the suction and then reposition her baby.

Frequency and length of feeds
Breast milk production (or lactation) is more easily established if the baby feeds within the first four hours after delivery. Each baby is an individual and it is inappropriate to force her into a feeding routine for an adult's convenience. In the first few weeks of life, breast-feeding babies often feed as frequently as every 1 to 2 hours.

Some babies will get all the milk they require within 5 minutes, while others will take longer. It is important to let the baby decide the length of the feed so that she gets the rich, high-fat 'hind' milk that will satisfy her for longer. Feeding on demand limits the chances of the breasts becoming engorged or overfull with milk.

It is not necessary for the baby to feed from both breasts at each feed. However, offering the other breast at the next feed would seem sensible.

BENEFITS TO THE BABY FROM BREAST-FEEDING

- Breast milk is suited to the baby's complete needs and digestion.
- It is almost germ-free (straight from producer to consumer!).
- The nutritional content of milk contains protective antibodies particularly effective against diarrhoea and vomiting. It is also thought to be helpful in the prevention of allergies.
- A breast-fed baby gets more cuddles from her mother.

BENEFITS TO THE MOTHER

- Breast-feeding is thought to aid the mother–child relationship.
- It is cheap.
- It is often less work when well-established.
- It aids in the contraction of the womb.
- It gives a sense of achievement of 'doing the best'.

BREAST-FEEDING DIFFICULTIES

Table 4.1 lists the common difficulties in breast-feeding and how they can be overcome.

Table 4.1   Common breast-feeding difficulties

Problem	Cause	Management

Sore nipples	a) Bad positioning
	b) Nipples constantly wet
	
	c) Infection such as thrush
		a) Check the baby's position at breast
		b) Expose nipples to air
		   Change breast pads frequently
		c) Treatment for both baby and
		   mother

Cracked nipples	Failure to manage sore nipples	Discontinue feeding Feed from other breast Keep dry Expose nipples to air Resume feeding

Engorgement (breasts over-full and painful)	a) Excess blood supply in
	   early days
	b) Poor positioning
	c) Inadequate removal of
	   milk from breasts
		a) Baby-led feeding
		   Bathing with hot and cold flannels
		b) Check feeding technique
		c) Use of firm bra
		   Possibly manual removal of small
		   amounts of milk

Blocked ducts (painful lumps in the breast, mother has no fever)	Poor feeding from baby or poor fixing	Correct fixing of the baby Regular, frequent feeds
Mastitis (infection or inflammation in a segment of the breast, possible fever)	Breast becoming overfull; inadequate feeding	Feed from affected side first Feed frequently Extra fluids to mother Bathe breasts with hot and cold flannels Possible treatment with antibiotics

continued

Table 4.1   Common breast-feeding difficulties *continued*

Problem	Cause	Management
Insufficient milk	a) Poor fixing	a) Check positioning
	b) Infrequent feeding	b) Baby-led feeding
	c) Use of complementary bottles	c) No bottles of milk
	d) Poorly nourished and overtired mother	d) Support mother, give good diet and sufficient fluids, check amounts of rest
Unsettled baby	Wet tired, abdominal pain; difficulty in fixing	Check physical comfort Additional support at feeding

Remember: What the mother eats will pass through her breast milk. This will include excess alcohol, all drugs and even nicotine.

Bottle-feeding

Cow's milk is ideal for calves, but it is not the natural food for babies. Bottled cow's milk, goat's milk and evaporated milk are unsuitable for babies under 6 months, and should preferably not to be given before 12 months, because:

- They contain high levels of the curd protein (see below), which is difficult to digest.
- The high salt content is potentially dangerous for the immature kidneys of infants.
- The fat content contains a higher proportion of fatty acids, which are poorly absorbed and can hinder calcium absorption.
- The iron from cow's milk is poorly absorbed.

Formula milks are recommended for babies in the first year of life who are not breast-fed. These are almost all cow's milk-based and have been changed by adapting the protein and fat contents and by supplementing extra vitamins and minerals. The addition of iron is particularly important.

WHICH MILK TO CHOOSE?

Formula milks are primarily whey- or curd-dominant. Whey-dominant formulae contain the protein lactalbumin, which is easy for a baby to digest. These milks are particularly suited to the new baby and are nearest in composition to breast milk.

Hungrier babies may be given curd-dominant formula which contains the protein casein. The curds in these milks take longer to digest and the baby feels fuller for longer.

However, there is no difference in the calorie, or nutrient content of the two types of milk.

From 6 to 12 months, 'follow-on' milks have been developed to be used in place of cow's milk. These are less modified than new baby milks but are again fortified with additional vitamins, iron and calcium.

Cow's milk intolerance
Some babies have difficulty in tolerating cow's milk products. This may be due to the specific protein or lactose (milk sugar) – see Chapter 6, page 86. As a result milks have been developed in which the proteins from soya bean have been used and the lactose has been changed to glucose. Medical advice should be sought prior to changing a baby to this type of formula to ensure that any symptoms are really due to an intolerance.

If soya-based milk is used, a baby may still develop a sensitivity to the protein. Care must also be taken with dental health as glucose is particularly harmful to healthy teeth – a cup should replace a bottle by 12 months to limit possible damage, if soya-based milk is used.

How to choose?
Advertising baby milks in the press or on television is forbidden by law. The biggest purchaser of baby milk is the National Health Service. As a result, mothers frequently continue with the milk their babies have been given in hospital.

Unless there is a strong reason to change, it is sensible for the baby to remain on this formula to allow her digestion and taste buds time to adjust. More information can be obtained from health visitors and baby clinics.

Activities

1 a) Visit a chemist's shop, or a specialist mother and baby shop, and research the different types of feeding bottles and teats that are available.
   b) Prepare a talk to your peers about the advantages and disadvantages of the different equipment you found.
   c) How can a new mother discover easily whether the manufacturers' claims are accurate?
2 Visit the local shops:
   a) What types of formula milk are available?
   b) Do they have age recommendations on them?
   c) Do they indicate if they are whey- or curd-based?
   d) Do you think the instructions for making up the feeds are adequate?
   e) Are all the instructions in English, or can you find any with instructions in different languages?
   f) Look at the packaging. What might affect a carer's choice between the brands?

PREPARATION OF FEEDS

Keeping things clean

Cleanliness is very important in the preparation of baby feeds. Germs live and breed in a warm food such as milk, so personal hygiene is vital.

All equipment should be sterile and surfaces cleaned with very hot soapy water. Sterilisation, usually using a chemical agent, means tanks and containers will need thorough washing every 24 hours and the correct concentration of solution made up (see the diagram below). Chemical sterilisation is preferable to boiling. However, if boiling is the chosen method, everything must be boiled under the water for a full 10 minutes. Steam sterilisers are effective and quick, but unfortunately still expensive.

1 Wash the bottles, teats and other equipment in hot water and detergent. Use a bottle brush for the inside of bottles. **Do not rub salt on the teats**. Squeeze boiled water through the teats.

2 Rinse everything thoroughly in clean running water

3 Fill the steriliser with clean, cold water. Add chemical solution. If in tablet form, allow to dissolve completely.

4 Put the bottles, teats and other equipment (nothing metal) into the water. Ensure everything is covered by the water, with no bubbles. If necessary, weight down. Leave for the required time according to manufacturer's instructions.

The procedure for sterilisation

What to do

The procedure fo preparing a bottle feed is shown in the diagram on page 58.

SAFE PRACTICE

- Always follow the guidelines for sterilisation and cleanliness.
- Feeds should be prepared in a kitchen away from other small children.
- Boiling liquids must never be passed over a small baby.
- Always check the milk temperature, before giving a baby a feed. A microwave oven is **not** suitable for the warming of bottles as they can produce unexpected 'hot spots'.

How much feed does a baby need?

The calculation for the nutritional needs of small babies is: 75 ml of fully reconstituted feed for every 500 g of the baby's weight in 24 hours ($2\frac{1}{2}$ fl. oz per lb of body weight $\times$ 24 hours). The total feed is then divided into the number of bottles it is likely the baby will take in that time. For a newborn, it is usually eight feeds.

REMEMBER!

- Every baby is an individual and, like breast-feeding, a schedule should be 'baby-led' to allow for changes in appetite.
- Inaccuracy in making up feeds is widespread.
- Over-concentration leads to excessive weight gain, too much salt and possible strain on the baby's kidneys.
- Cereals and sugars should never be added to bottles.
- Under-concentration is less common, but it can lead to poor weight gain, constipation and a distressed, hungry baby.

PROCEDURE FOR GIVING A BOTTLE

- Wash your hands.
- Collect all equipment for the feed, before picking up the baby. Place the bottle on a tray and cover it. Keep it warm in a jug of hot water. Put the bib, tissues and any other articles ready too.
- Change the baby and make her comfortable. Wash your hands.
- Take the baby to the feeding area and sit in a comfortable position. This is a time for talking and cuddling the baby, and should be enjoyable, for both of you, not to be rushed. Maintain eye contact and hold the baby firmly to give her a sense of security
- Test the temperature of the milk against the inside of your wrist.
- Test the size of the teat by turning the bottle upside down. The milk should flow freely at first – several drops per second.

1 Check that the formula has not passed its sell-by date. Read the instructions on the tin. Ensure the tin has been kept in a cool, dry cupboard.

2 Boil some **fresh** water and allow to cool.

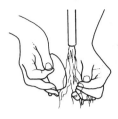

3 Wash hands and nails thoroughly.

4 Take required equipment from sterilising tank and rinse with cool, boiled water.

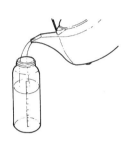

5 Fill bottle, or a jug if making a large quantity, to the required level with water.

6 Measure the **exact** amount of powder using the scoop provided. Level with a knife. **Do not pack down.**

7 Add the powder to the measured water in the bottle or jug.

8 Screw cap on bottle and shake, or mix well in the jug and pour into sterilised bottles.

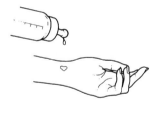

9 If not using immediately, **cool quickly** and store in the fridge. If using immediately, test temperature on the inside of your wrist.

10 Babies will take cold milk but they prefer warm food (as from the breast). If you wish to warm the milk, place bottle in a jug of hot water. **Never keep warm for longer than 45 minutes** to reduce chances of bacteria breeding.

Preparing a bottle feed

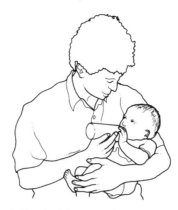

The baby should be held securely, with good eye contact

- Stimulate the rooting reflex, by gently touching the baby's lips with the teat and then place the teat over her tongue and into her mouth.
- Check that milk is always present in the teat. This stops the baby sucking on air and becoming frustrated at not receiving feed. Gentle tension on the teat helps the baby to keep sucking steadily.
- A feed usually takes about 20 minutes with a break after about 10 minutes to bring up the baby's wind (see below). After a feed, let the wind come up again.
- Change the baby again, if necessary, and settle her comfortably and safely.
- Clear away, wash utensils thoroughly and re-sterilise.

REMEMBER!

- A baby should **never** be propped up with a bottle.
- Choking can easily occur.
- Siblings and unsure adults will need supervision at all times when feeding.
- Bottles are for milk or cooled boiled water – **never** add solids.

WINDING A BABY

Many old wive's tales are linked with bringing up a baby's wind.
- Air rises naturally in an upright bottle, so the baby too should be held upright. This helps nature.
- Apply gentle, but firm pressure to the baby's stomach. This can be by the heel of your hand if the baby is on the your lap, or by the front of the your body if you are standing.
- Gently rub the baby's back.

This should result in natural winding.

If winding does not take place within a few seconds, it will mean that the air has continued down the gastric tract and will be expelled in the nappy. Babies often release wind without any help and only become distressed with an adult's efforts to help.

IS THE BABY HAVING ENOUGH FOOD?

This is a question often asked by anxious carers, whether the baby is breast- or bottle-fed. Consider the following when deciding:

- appearance and general behaviour
- weight gain – this should be 130–170 g (6–8 oz) per week for the first four months (breast-fed babies lose more weight after birth than bottle-fed babies, but this is made up by 10 to 14 days)
- alertness when awake, and falling asleep following a period of calm, after a feed
- warm and silky skin, firm and elastic to touch
- pink mucous membranes
- abdomen prominent after feeds, but not distended
- whether the baby moves and kicks well, cries for food, (or if cold or insecure), but does not have prolonged crying spells
- sleeps well between feeds
- urine and stools passed easily without discomfort.

REMEMBER!

- Bottle-fed babies' stools are putty coloured, formed and faecal smelling.
- Breast-fed babies stools are inoffensive, mustard-coloured and very soft.

Weighing

While this is an important sign of growth and sufficient food, remember that babies will have spurts in gaining weight.

Variation in the times of day the baby is weighed, the accuracy of the scales, variations between scales, whether the baby is clothed or naked, whether the baby is weighed before or after a feed, will all play a part in differences and unexpected changes in weight.

Weaning

When a baby is no longer satisfied with breast or formula milk and is taking large quantities of fluids, then weaning (the introduction of solid food) might be considered. COMA recommendations are that this should not be before the age of 4 months and not later than 6 months.

By 4 months a baby's kidney function is sufficiently mature to cope with natural salt in weaning foods. The digestive enzymes, gastric acid, and the absorptive capacities of the small and large bowel, are ready to manage solid foods. Also, by 4 months the baby is able to hold up her head, swallow food and move it to the back of the mouth. If solid food is not introduced by 6 months this key developmental stage may be missed and chewing difficulties and food refusal may occur.

Weaning should be a gentle, on-going learning process that the baby and her carer undertake together – it should never be a battleground.

AIMS OF WEANING

- To make the baby less nutritionally dependent on milk. By the age of 12 months, milk should provide about 40 per cent of the calorie intake. So it still remains an important food source for the toddler.
- To provide a variety of textures, purees and dices which will enable the baby to join in family meals, so aiding her social and intellectual development.
- To establish the acceptance of a variety of foods and flavours, setting healthy eating patterns throughout childhood.
- To introduce iron into the diet. Human and unfortified cow's milks are poor sources of this mineral.
- To introduce a cup and spoon to the baby to encourage and stimulate her independence.

MANAGING THE WEANING PROCESS

Many mothers worry about this aspect of child rearing, so it is especially important that you, as a child care worker, are calm and confident. It helps to remember that the nutritional content of early weaning is less important than the baby beginning to learn about, and accept, different flavours and textures.

As with any learning experience the baby should not be too tired or even too hungry. She has yet to realise that the spoon will satisfy her as the bottle or breast does.

Milk can be given before a feed to help settle a hungry baby. Allow plenty of time for this new experience to promote a relaxed atmosphere. The morning or early afternoon feeds are good times for introducing something new.

At first, offer a half to one teaspoon of a bland, warm savoury food. The spoon must be sterilised and the best one is plastic with a flat bowl that allows the baby to suck the contents off easily. Ideally, first weaning foods should be gluten-free, sugar-free, salt-free and have a sloppy consistency, for example baby rice, mashed potato or banana, mixed with formula or breast milk.

After this initial introduction the same food can be offered the next day. Too many tastes at one time can confuse a small baby and if something upsets her it is easier to discover the cause. Refusal may not mean dislike of the food itself, but of the new experience.

After two to three days when the baby is used to the new flavour and consistency, another food can be tried. If the first chosen weaning food is a baby cereal, the next food could be a puréed fruit or vegetable. Babies appear to enjoy the very bland nature of cereals and there is a risk of a baby becoming overweight if too much is given.

Eggs can be used in weaning, towards the latter part of the first year, but only if both white and yolk are cooked to solid consistency to limit the risk of Salmonella.

As the quantity of solid food a baby eats increases, the amounts of milk offered may be gradually reduced so that by about the fifth week of weaning one of the milk feeds can be completely replaced by solids. As this happens the baby's thirst should be quenched with cooled, boiled water. Diluted freshly squeezed fruit juices can be offered too, but only in a cup, never in a bottle.

Babies do not need teeth to cope with more lumpy foods, as they use their hard back gums to manage lumps, and from about 7 months pieces of hard foods such as crusts, peeled apple or carrot can be given.

As the baby becomes more actively involved, let her 'help' by holding a spoon as well. She will discover the textures and temperatures of her food with her fingers, as well as developing the co-ordination required to get food into her mouth. This is usually great fun and inevitably messy, so plan accordingly with bibs and floor protection

REMEMBER!

Learning to manage lumps, experiencing different tastes and textures, developing hand–eye skills and eating in family groups are just as important as the nutritional aspect of weaning.

SAFE PRACTICE

Supervision remains vital, especially when changes in food consistency are introduced. Always consider this at mealtimes.

WEANING PLANS

A suggested weaning plan is shown in Table 4.2.

Table 4.2 A suggested weaning plan

Age/months	4 months	4½ months	5–6 months	6–7 months	7–8 months	9–12 months
On waking	Breast or bottle feed	Breast or bottle feed	Breast or bottle feed	Breast or bottle feed	Breast or bottle feed	Breast or bottle feed/cup
Breakfast	1–2 teaspoon baby rice mixed with milk from feed or with water; breast or bottle feed	2 teaspoon baby rice mixed with milk from feed or with water; breast or bottle feed	Baby rice or cereal mixed with milk from feed or with water or pureed banana; breast or bottle feed	Cereal mixed with milk from feed or water; fruit, toast fingers spread with unsalted butter	Cereal, fish or fruit; toast fingers; milk	Cereal and milk; fish, yoghurt or fruit; toast and milk
Lunch	Breast or bottle feed	1–2 teaspoon puree or sieved vegetables or vegetables and chicken; breast or bottle feed	Pureed or sieved meat or fish and vegetables, or proprietary food; followed by 2 teaspoon pureed fruit or prepared baby dessert; drink of cooled, boiled water or well-diluted juice (from a cup)	Finely minced meat or mashed fish, with mashed vegetables; mashed banana or stewed fruit or milk pudding; drink of cooled boiled water or well-diluted juice in a cup	Mashed fish, minced meat or cheese with vegetables; milk pudding or stewed fruit; drink	Well-chopped meat, liver or fish or cheese with mashed vegetables; milk pudding or fruit fingers; drink
Tea	Breast or bottle feed	Breast or bottle feed	Pureed fruit or baby dessert; breast or bottle feed	Toast with cheese or savoury spread; breast or bottle feed	Bread and butter sandwiches with savoury spread or seedless jam; sponge finger or biscuit; milk drink	Fish, cheese or pasta; sandwiches; fruit; milk drink
Late evening	Breast or bottle feed	Breast or bottle feed	Breast or bottle feed, if necessary			

REMEMBER!

- Is the baby comfortable?
- Is the baby well-supervised?
- Remove bib after meals.
- No salt or sugar.
- Check temperature of food carefully – no blowing!
- Check for any bones in fish.

Activity

As a professional child care worker you will be expected to have wide knowlege to meet the needs of a variety of different families.

1 Make three weaning plans (see Table 4.2) for babies in your care. These plans should be for the first year of life and should demonstrate the changes the baby will encounter during her first year in sucking, chewing and coping with lumps, etc.
   a) Make one plan for a baby whose parents wish her to be a vegetarian.
   b) Make one plan for a baby whose parents are Asian Muslims.
   c) Make one plan for a baby whose parents are of Afro-Carribean origin.

You will need to research widely the dietary and nutritional requirements of each of these plans. Visit libraries, child health cinics, the health visiting service and community dietician for information.

REMEMBER!

4–6 months offer sieved or pureed food
6–8 months offer mashed and finger foods
8–9 months offer chopped foods

2 How do you think the foods in the plans you made above might differ from the weaning plan in Table 4.2?
3 How easily could you meet the cultural and religious wishes of these families?
4 Did you find that baby food manufacturers are responsive to the needs of the variety of customs and cultures in our society?
5 Check and comment on the nutritional content of commercial baby foods from their labels. Take notice of any 'hidden' sugars or salt.
6 Write a report justifying for your selections, based on cost, nutritional needs and parental choices. Did you find it difficult to meet these needs?

Possible feeding difficulties

Table 4.3 lists the main problems associated with feeding and how they may be managed.

Table 4.3   Problems associated with feeding

Problem	Signs and symptoms	Management
Allergies and intolerances	Failure to thrive, diarrhoea and vomiting, infantile eczema/general rashes, wheezing	Liaise with medical advice/dietician Breast-feed if possible Use cow's milk replacement, for example, soya milk
Constipation	Small, hard, infrequent stools	Increase fluid intake Ensure feed not too concentrated No laxatives or sugar in feeds If weaned, increase fruit or vegetable intake. Check to exclude underfeeding
Diarrhoea	Frequent, loose watery stools	Check hygiene of food preparation Give clear fluids and seek medical advice
Colic	Babies of (usually) less than 3 months cry and draw legs up appearing to have abdominal pain. Often showing distress at the same time of day – frequently early evening	Cause unknown Feed baby Check teat for size and flow, if bottle-fed Monitor feeding technique Reassure carer that pain is self-limiting Comfort baby with movement and cuddling Seek advice from health visitor
Overfeeding	Baby vomits/unsettled, passes large stools, sore buttocks, excessive weight gain	Seek clinic/health visitor advice Check re-constitution of feeds
Possetting	Baby frequently vomits small amounts, but gains weight and is happy	Condition self-limiting usually solved when baby is upright and walking Monitor weight
Underfeeding	Baby very hungry, wakes and cries; stools small and dark, poor weight gain; vomiting as a result of crying and air swallowing	Ensure feeds are correctly re-constituted If breast-feeding, check technique and mother's diet Increase frequency of feeds, before quantities

REMEMBER!

Diarrhoea and vomiting can be serious in small babies, whatever the reason, and medical advice should be sought.

QUICK CHECK

1 Describe the nutritional advantages to an infant of breast-feeding.
2 How can the successful production of breast milk be undermined?
3 A mother complains her nipples are sore when breast-feeding. What advice might you offer?
4 Which mineral is stored in the baby's liver for use during the first few months of life?
5 A mother asks how much weight her new baby should be gaining. How would you reply?
6 How would you reassure a mother who is worried that her breast milk, after four weeks breast-feeding, looks watery?
7 A mother bottle-feeding a 4–week-old baby asks how much feed should be offered. What would you answer?
8 Describe the main hygiene principles that must be used for safe bottle-feeding.
9 What specific safety factors should be remembered when weaning a baby?
10 What might lead you to suspect that a baby was being underfed?
11 How could you help a baby who was having colic?
12 'Weaning is a learning process.' Explain what you understand by this.
13 A baby of 5 months persistently rejects food offered on a spoon. What might be the reasons?
14 Why is a microwave oven unsuitable for warming babies' bottles?
15 Describe how a baby who is being bottle-fed should be held.

KEY WORDS AND TERMS

You need to know what these words and phrases mean. Go back through the chapter and find out.

designer food
colostrum
fixing at the breast
areola
let-down reflex
supply and demand of milk
fore and hind milk
lactose
engorgement
mastitis
blocked ducts

whey- and curd-dominant formula
soya milk
microwave 'hot spots'
COMA weaning age recommendations
times for puréed, mashed and
chopped foods
possetting
colic
signs of underfeeding.

5 FEEDING THE GROWING CHILD

> **This chapter covers:**
> ■ **Mealtimes for children**
> ■ **Feeding toddlers**
> ■ **Feeding children with special needs**
> ■ **Preventing food fads and minor eating problems**

Mealtimes for children

The issue of food carries with it both power and emotion. A mother who lovingly shops for organic foods, prepares, cooks and presents a healthy meal to a toddler may understandably find if difficult to be relaxed if he spits it out. She may feel as rejected as the food.

When feeding small children, the person who provides the food is also likely to be the controller of what is offered. So, if a carer dislikes vegetables and fresh fruits, for example, he or she may either not provide them or give out hidden messages to a small child that they are 'not good'. Never expect a small child to eat what you will not eat yourself. Also, if a carer's own knowledge of basic nutrition is limited, he or she may inadvertently offer a poorly balanced diet.

We therefore bring our own eating patterns to feeding children. Do any of the following remind you of your childhood?

Cost governed the food offered, for example lots of fatty cheap, filling foods.

A sweet if you are good.

Eat up for mummy.

No tea if you are naughty.

Manners were everything.

Everyone always ate too much.

Meals were always hurried.

A sweet to take the pain away.

No one would eat anything different.

So food is much more complex than just providing fuel for the body. It can become a sign to the outside world of a 'good' carer. To some people, this will be a bouncing, large child, while to others it would mean a slim, possibly underweight, child. Carers often boast that their children 'will eat everything'. Others may be reluctant to let their children go to parties where there might be 'junk food' and so limit a child's opportunity for social development.

Whatever our backgrounds and previous experiences, it is difficult to be calm about food and children.

CHANGING PATTERNS

Our eating habits have changed over the years. Why?
- We have more labour-saving machinery.
- We are less active, using cars and buses more, and as a result can more easily become overweight.
- Modern technology means we can have almost any food all year round, for example, strawberries, mangoes, kiwi fruit.
- We are busy and have less time to shop, cook and eat our foods, especially in a relaxed family setting.
- As a nation we eat too many fatty and sugary foods from convenience sources.

This all affects how we plan and organise food for children.

Mealtime can be a wonderful opportunity for a family or nursery to have a pleasurable time together – perhaps to discuss the day's events, learn new words, have new experiences and develop healthy attitudes to food.

Most children respond to a regular routine of mealtimes and constant snacking ('grazing') can be detrimental to a healthy appetite, limiting the opportunity for eating important body-building foods.

REMEMBER!

- A snack to an adult may be the equivalent of a meal to a child.
- Check that food is not used instead of attention, for example giving a child a packet of crisps to eat while watching TV.
- Avoid using food as a bribe or a reward.
- The adult is a role model in diet.
- Small children need three meals a day and usually two or three small healthy snacks. See Chapter 3, page 31.

ᴺ TO EAT

ᶠ meals is important. A child may be too tired to take advantage of ᵥᵥy meal at the end of the day. A main meal at midday is preferable, plus ᵗne usual recommended snacks – children need regular 'fuel' during the day to cope with their activity.

Meals should not be hurried. A child at nursery is learning new skills of handling cutlery, tasting new foods and textures, extending his language and being introduced to the social custom of group eating. He may start by eating his favourite or known food and be rushed into leaving what may be more important nutritionally. He may use different utensils at home or come from a culture where eating with fingers is the norm. All children may be faced with unfamiliar foods and smells, and time is needed to help them to respond to new situations.

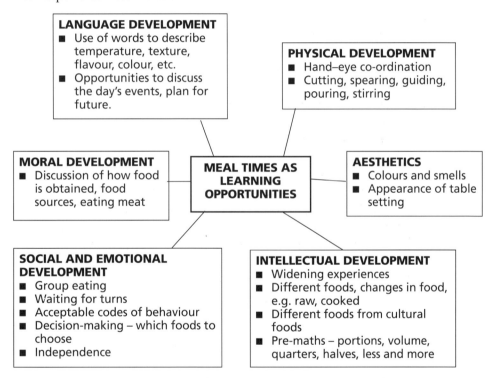

LANGUAGE DEVELOPMENT
- Use of words to describe temperature, texture, flavour, colour, etc.
- Opportunities to discuss the day's events, plan for future.

PHYSICAL DEVELOPMENT
- Hand–eye co-ordination
- Cutting, spearing, guiding, pouring, stirring

MORAL DEVELOPMENT
- Discussion of how food is obtained, food sources, eating meat

MEAL TIMES AS LEARNING OPPORTUNITIES

AESTHETICS
- Colours and smells
- Appearance of table setting

SOCIAL AND EMOTIONAL DEVELOPMENT
- Group eating
- Waiting for turns
- Acceptable codes of behaviour
- Decision-making – which foods to choose
- Independence

INTELLECTUAL DEVELOPMENT
- Widening experiences
- Different foods, changes in food, e.g. raw, cooked
- Different foods from cultural foods
- Pre-maths – portions, volume, quarters, halves, less and more

GOOD PRACTICE

- Meal times should be relaxed and unhurried.
- Food should be set out attractively.
- Children eat best in company.
- Encourage hand washing before mealtimes.

- Offer a variety of foods, and foods from different cultures.
- Try not to overfill plates. It is best to offer seconds.
- Children's appetites vary.
- Consider the timing of the main meal.
- Tiredness and illness can affect appetites. Exercise can stimulate it.
- Offer water at meal times.
- Encourage careful eating and cutlery use, but do not over-emphasise – it is best to learn from adult example.
- Foods refused can frequently be reintroduced later.
- Nutritional needs can be met in a variety of ways.
- Allow children some choice.
- Occasional sweets and junk foods do no harm.
- Food should never be used as a punishment.

REMEMBER!

It is easier to form healthy attitudes to food than to change poor habits.

Activity
Planning for lunch time
a) Ask the nursery children to design a table cloth, either by decorating a paper one or by painting or printing a plain sheet. Suggest they choose a colour or topic theme.
b) Decorate napkins and paper beakers to match.
c) Illustrate menus, for example with pictures of different foods.
d) Arrange posies of flowers for centre pieces.
e) Set the table with accuracy.

Feeding toddlers

The nutritional principles in feeding toddlers are the same as for all young children, including full involvement in family food and meal times.

REMEMBER!

- Small, regular, high quality meals – between 1200 and 1400 kcal daily.
- One pint of whole milk daily.
- Vitamin supplements A, D and C.
- Monitor iron intakes.
- Gradual introduction to wider foods and textures, including spices and pulses.

- No added salt or sugar.
- Only ground nuts until the age of 4. Check for peanut allergy.

Between the ages of 1 and 2 a child is rapidly developing new skills and is keen to use them. Although he will be able to use a spoon, he may drop food or turn the spoon over before it reaches his mouth.

The toddler is rapidly developing new skills and is keen to practise them

A child will use his fingers to supplement spoons. He may spill his drink. The language he has to illustrate and explain his needs is limited – 50 to 100 words by 2 years. However his understanding is much wider. He is aware of his developing power over his world and is keen to gain independence. All this means that meal times can be demanding for carers and possibly frustrating for the toddler.

Plan for mess and ensure the toddler is secure in a harness in his high chair. Try to provide equipment to aid his independence, such as flat-bowled spoons, plastic bowls fixed by suction to the high chair trays and beakers with two handles. He may still need a bottle for comfort at bed time, but only for water or milk. However, by the age of 2 many children no longer use bottles. Feeding beakers are unneccessary as they require a sucking action rather than teaching a drinking action. Drinks given in an egg cup during bath time can help the child to practise adult drinking and make spills easier to manage – not the bath water though!

Allow the toddler to practise his emerging skills – it will take time and tolerance. Even if he appears inefficient at feeding himself, he is gaining valuable skills and experience. Taking over may provoke frustration and a negative response from him. He is finding that he has choice and power and a 'No' from a toddler at meal times will not be changed by food being forced on him. It is both professionally unacceptable and probably unsuccessful – even if food reaches his mouth, he will be unlikely to swallow it and this may even lead to a more serious long-term eating problem.

As with older children, a toddler enjoys eating in company and occasionally from his carer's plate. He learns partly by imitation and will be less likely to encroach on an adult's plate if he is allowed to have time experimenting with the process of eating from his own plate or bowl. This may mean feeling the texture and temperature of foods with his fingers, testing the consistency and occasionally seeing if food fits in his ears and nose too!

Allow the toddler to feel the texture and temperature of foods with his fingers

As long as the carer expects this and tries to be relaxed, never forcing food or displaying disgust at mess, this can be thought of as a normal development.

A toddler may have periods of food refusal, spitting out what were previously accepted foods and showing a reluctance to sit at the table. Here he is demonstrating his developing power over his own environment and understanding how to use it. A positive response is to accept it as a 'phase' and ensure that he is not filling up on inappropriate snacks, that meal timings are suitable and accept that he will eat when he is hungry. Unacceptable foods should not be hidden in other, preferred foods as this undermines trust and may result in familiar and nutritious foods being discarded.

Avoid battles over food – they prolong the situation and mealtimes can then become distressing for everyone. A carer can never make a child eat and, if food is forced upon him, the child may not swallow it or may even vomit. He can miss the odd meal and still remain healthy, and he will always eat when he is hungry.

SAFE PRACTICE

- Chewing may be hurried or immature, so always check for hard lumps, bones and any whole nuts – **supervise**.
- Never leave a toddler unattended – secure him with a fixed harness in a high chair.
- Do not use drinking glasses as pieces can be bitten out.
- Always check the temperature of food.

Feeding children with special needs

Some children, particularly those with cerebral palsy, may have problems in eating. These difficulties can become more pronounced when solid foods are introduced. Such a child may have difficulties with swallowing and in releasing his bite and grasp reflexes. In addition, he may experience spasms of the neck muscles, with arching of the back, which makes positioning difficult.

An inability to cope with either the amount or the consistency of a food may lead to choking. So when new types of food are introduced, it should be done slowly and gradually, with supervision and a knowledge of first aid. Finger foods and foods of a sloppy consistency are best to start with, gradually moving to foods of a firmer texture. Try not to have foods that break easily, such as crumbly biscuits.

Adjust the child's sitting position before a meal so his head is in midline with his arms stretched across the table and his feet flat on the floor or on the high chair foot support. Place the cutlery on the table or tray so he can try to pick them up. Sit at his side and help him only if needed, encourage his independence and praise his effort.

GOOD PRACTICE

Even though mealtimes may take longer, it is important for the child's self-esteem to learn to feed himself, if possible. All children benefit from the handling of food – learning texture, consistency, shape and temperature. Children with special needs also gain from this sensory experience.

Children with special needs also have likes and dislikes, and variations in appetite.

USEFUL EQUIPMENT

- Tough plastic spoons with large, rounded handles.
- Heavy, flat, round feeding dishes with wide bases.
- Non-slip mats to prevent equipment sliding.
- Two-handled mugs.
- Weighted trainer mugs (readily available from chemists).
- Straws – these are sometimes are easier to manage than a mug or a cup.

As with any child, encouragement, a pleasant atmosphere and company help to make meal times enjoyable. If the child has to be fed, again ensure he is sitting correctly and comfortably. Feed him slowly and carefully, especially if he has poor control of his throat muscles and there is a risk of choking. Cut the food into small pieces and place it on the back of his tongue to ease swallowing. Check for hard lumps, fish bones, etc. Always tell the child what you are giving him.

Mouth hygiene is important and should be included in the daily routine. Teeth cleaning provides an opportunity for enhancing an awareness of the lips, tongue and teeth. Rinsing and spitting out is a good exercise for weak lip and tongue muscles.

Preventing food fads and minor eating problems

As we have already said, nutrition for small children is an emotive issue for many carers. It provokes feelings of inadequacy and rejection when difficulties occur. Setting and developing good habits are much easier than attempting to change entrenched eating patterns.

A child who has previously eaten well can show sudden upset when there are changes in his life. New schools, new babies, illnesses and temporary separation from prime carers can all upset a child's eating pattern, which usually settles of its own accord if not over-stressed. Knowing about such changes can help you to manage any feeding problems. Try not to introduce unfamiliar foods at these times.

An over-emphasis on table manners and a reluctance to allow toddlers to make a mess when eating can lead to food refusal. Sometimes a carer may be unaware that small children can be messy when eating and feel that his or her child is abnormal. If a child eats on his own, he may wish to finish as quickly as possible in order to rejoin his friends and so may develop a poor appetite.

REMEMBER!

- Children's appetites vary.
- Children have food likes and dislikes which should be respected.
- It is important to distinguish between the child who needs less food than the average and the child who refuses food as a part of his growing independence. A balanced diet can usually be achieved by meeting nutritional needs from other food sources, for example yoghurt instead of cheese for calcium.

It is important to praise and encourage a child trying new and different foods. If he is experiencing minor eating difficulties, a negative attitude to these new foods may otherwise develop. Older children can be encouraged by involving them in shopping, cooking and setting tables as well as some choice in menu selection.

Carers keen on 'healthy' diets need to ensure that no undue emphasis is placed on specific foods, for example by identifying foods as 'good' or 'bad', such as white versus brown bread. Toddlers in particular will sense any emotional tension from carers during mealtimes. A matter-of-fact approach to food fads and refusal is usually most effective.

Ensure that food is not used to replace attention – a story at the end of the day rather than a chocolate bar will be more beneficial to a child's development.

It is interesting that some children identified as having eating problems manage quite happily in a group situation away from the emotional tension of anxious carers.

DO YOU NEED HELP?

These are signs that you should seek professional help with an eating problem:
- The child is not gaining weight.
- The child does not reach his milestones of development and is not happy and sociable.
- The child is not fit, lacks energy and suffers from recurrent illness (see Failure to thrive, Chapter 8).

Where to seek help
The health visitor and GP would usually be able to advise on minor food problems and meal management. If the difficulties become serious you will be referred to a Child Guidance Clinic and psychological help may be sought.

QUICK CHECK

1 What do you understand by the phrase 'food as a power tool'?
2 List five ways in which our eating patterns have changed over the last 20 years.
3 Explain the term 'grazing'.
4 Explain what you understand by 'Meal times are a learning experience.'
5 What can affect a child's appetite?
6 What are the special nutritional requirements for a toddler?
7 Why would a knowledge of first aid be important when feeding children with special needs?
8 How do toddlers learn to develop acceptable meal-time behaviour?
9 How would you manage a toddler's food fads?
10 List the signs that would indicate that a child is not thriving.
11 How can carers pass on negative attitudes to food?
12 What choice of cutlery would help a child with special needs to develop independence in feeding?
13 Where could a carer go for dietary advice for a child who has feeding difficulties?
14 What do understand by 'finger feeding'?
15 What safety procedures should you implement when feeding toddlers?

KEY WORDS AND TERMS

You need to know what these words and phrases mean. Go back through the chapter and find out.

eating habits
food and emotion/power
finger feeding

negative response
food refusal

6 INFLUENCES ON FOOD AND DIET

> **This chapter covers:**
> - **School meals**
> - **The food industry and the media**
> - **Poverty**
> - **Food allergies and intolerances**

School meals

Cooked school meals were first introduced in 1906 with the aim of improving the nutritional status of poor people. To begin with the meals were supplied for just three days a week and often only during winter. In the 1940s, cooked school meals became available as a right for any child who wanted one. This meal was intended to be a child's main meal of the day and was intended to provide one third of the daily requirements of protein, energy and some vitamins and minerals. The price of these meals was strictly controlled. In addition, free milk was available for all school children.

However, various Education Acts have since brought about major changes in the legislation (laws) governing school meals:

- In 1980, national nutritional standards and price controls were abolished.
- Also in 1980, free school milk for all children was withdrawn, although some primary schools continue to purchase milk at subsidised prices.
- In 1986, schools had to put the supply of meal services out to competitive tender.
- In 1988, many children lost their eligibility for free meals.
- Also in 1988, some payments were replaced by direct cash sums to families, which could or could not be spent on food.
- In 1990, LEAs (Local Education Authorities) were only required to provide meals for children entitled to free dinners and to provide a place for children to eat packed lunches.

Some LEAs now only provide meals for children who are are eligible for free school meal (a 'meal' need only be a sandwich).

THE EFFECTS OF CHANGES IN LEGISLATION

The main effects are:

■ School meals now cost more as there is pressure for profits to be made (meals come out of the Education budget).

■ In an attempt to cut down on waste and offer children greater choice, cafeteria systems have become more widespread. However, this is thought to encourage children to choose unbalanced meals. Research shows that there is a better balance of nutrients in 'traditional' school meals.

■ The meals provided are increasingly high in fats and sugars and low in iron. Girls are particularly at risk as a third are iron-deficient by the age of 11.

Other difficulties connected with school meals include:

■ inadequate time for lunch, especially where classrooms are used as dining rooms

■ lack of parental/carer awareness of what children are eating at lunch time

■ poor guidance to smaller children – an unappealing main course may result in a child only eating fatty or sugary foods – chips or pudding

■ lack of suitable choices of meals for children from minority groups.

School cafeterias are thought to encourage children to choose unbalanced meals

Activity

a) Record how many children in your infant school placement have cooked school meals.

b) Assess the nutritional content.
c) Compare what is offered and what is actually eaten. Is sufficient calcium, iron and vitamin A provided?
d) How many meals are hot? How long are meals kept hot? Does this affect the vitamin content?
e) Is there choice? If so, is there choice for children who are vegetarian or who come from different ethnic backgrounds?

PACKED LUNCHES – THE ALTERNATIVE TO SCHOOL MEALS

The advantage of packed lunches is that their contents can be controlled by the carer. The disadvantage, however, is that the carer may not know exactly what his or her child has eaten.

The advantage of school meals, on the other hand, is that small children often will eat unfamiliar foods when in the company of friends having the same. School dinners can also provide opportunities for widening experiences outside the family. This is lost in packed lunches.

Packed lunches often provide only cold food – an important consideration for the younger child. Many carers leading busy lives find packed meals time-consuming to make. Studies have shown that infant school children prefer their lunch boxes to contain:

■ strong tastes
■ hard, crispy textures
■ items at room temperature or frozen
■ interesting shapes for the food or its container
■ 'finger foods' of bite size.

Activities
1 Plan a week's packed lunches for a 6-year-old during the summer term.
   ■ Choose from a variety of foods from the five food groups.
   ■ Consider the reseach mentioned above.
   ■ Include two healthy snacks and unflavoured milk or water to drink.
   ■ Look for hidden sugars in any bought foods
   ■ Remember the energy needs of a 6-year-old.
   ■ Ensure that the foods you choose transport well.
2 Plan an alternative week's lunches for a child who is vegetarian, using the same criteria as in activity 1.
   What sources of iron and B-group vitamins would you choose?

3 Cost both sets of lunches and compare with the prices of traditional or cafeteria dinners at your placement.
4 Which lunches do you consider best meet the child's nutritional needs?

SAFE PRACTICE

- Food may remain in lunch boxes for long periods, increasing the risk of bacterial food poisoning.
- Prepare any sandwiches or rolls at the last minute, or make and freeze in batches.
- Use insulated cool bags for transport.

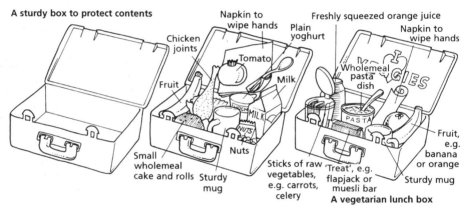

Examples of nutritious lunch boxes

Activity

Design a healthy eating campaign for an infant school, linking classroom learning to encouraging healthier lunchtime choices.

- Include information about how to choose healthier food and drinks – perhaps colour-coded menus or stars for foods you wish to promote.
- Think about how you could involve parents or carers in the campaign. Perhaps you could hold a 'tasting' evening of foods from the current menu.
- Think about how you could promote a multi-cultural food policy.

The food industry and the media

Besides home and school, there are many other influences on children's eating habits, and they are becoming increasingly sophisticated. They can be obvious, such as the popular birthday party facilities at fast-food restaurants. Children keen to be the same as their peers can put strong pressure on parents and carers to hold such parties.

There are other, more subtle influences of which we may be unaware. For example, displays in supermarkets and the placing of sweets, crisps, etc. on the shelves can be very tempting for toddlers. Even more so if these items are placed at checkouts where a fraught mother may be queueing to pay, accompanied by a bored child who wants the sweets and chocolates on display.

Packaging, advertisements and the images they promote frequently portray ideas of health, success and happiness – usually in stable, traditional family settings with highly-involved fathers. Breakfasts always seem to be civilised with families sitting around tables with plenty of time, and with everyone even-tempered!

Cans of soft drinks often promote images of amazing athletic or sporting success. Some brands of foods offer additional reasons for parents and carers to buy them again, for example free games, gifts or cards to collect may be included, or offers of reduced prices on future purchases. All of these make it difficult for parents and carers to make decisions solely for nutritional reasons.

In addition, nutritional information included on packaging can be confusing and technical, for example glucose, fructose, sucrose are all basically sugars – but which is 'best'?

When shopping, various influences can affect your decisions on what to puchase:

- price
- taste
- image – television, packaging, magazines
- nutritional value.

Poverty

We have seen that school meal prices are increasing and that the nutritional value of these meals may be decreasing. This means that families must take responsibility for ensuring children are well-fed with nutritious food to promote healthy development.

A survey carried out by NCH Action for Children in 1994 found that parents receiving state benefits experience difficulty in providing nutritionally balanced meals on small incomes. The findings of the survey were:

- Parents frequently go without food to ensure their children do not.
- Two-thirds of children in families on benefit were eating what nutritionists describe as a 'poor diet'.
- The average money spent on food was under £10 per person per week (the national average is over £13). For families on benefit this meant that the money spent on food could be up to 35 per cent of total household costs.

COST DIFFERENCES BETWEEN 'HEALTHY' AND 'UNHEALTHY' DIETS

The average cost of a 'healthy' shopping basket was £5 per week more than the 'unhealthy' one. Prices increase in rural areas where shopping for bargains is difficult. Transport problems often mean reliance on an inevitably more expensive local shop.

There is no evidence to show that poorer families offer less healthy diets because they are unaware of what should be provided, it is just that they do not have the money. Cheap, filling foods, such as chips and pies, provide energy, but fruit, vegetables and iron-rich foods are expensive, yet necessary for growing children. As a result, children in families with low incomes are found to have diets high in saturated fats and sugars and low in vitamins, minerals and iron.

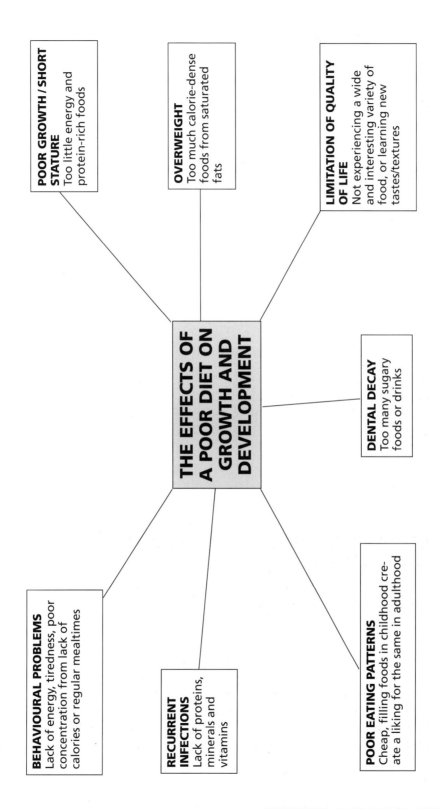

POOR GROWTH / SHORT STATURE
Too little energy and protein-rich foods

OVERWEIGHT
Too much calorie-dense foods from saturated fats

LIMITATION OF QUALITY OF LIFE
Not experiencing a wide and interesting variety of food, or learning new tastes/textures

THE EFFECTS OF A POOR DIET ON GROWTH AND DEVELOPMENT

DENTAL DECAY
Too many sugary foods or drinks

BEHAVIOURAL PROBLEMS
Lack of energy, tiredness, poor concentration from lack of calories or regular mealtimes

RECURRENT INFECTIONS
Lack of proteins, minerals and vitamins

POOR EATING PATTERNS
Cheap, filling foods in childhood create a liking for the same in adulthood

CHEAP SOURCES OF ENERGY AND NUTRIENTS

- **Energy:** lard, margarine, vegetable oil, white bread, old potatoes, pasta, breakfast cereals
- **Protein:** liver, eggs, baked beans, cheese, milk, rice chicken
- **Carbohydrate:** sugar, white bread, potatoes, pasta, biscuits, ice cream,
- **Iron:** liver, fortified breakfast cereals, wholemeal bread
- **Vitamin A:** liver, carrots, margarine, eggs, milk, cheese
- **Thiamin:** fortified breakfast cereals, old potatoes, wholemeal bread, pork, liver, bacon, ham
- **Riboflavin:** liver, breakfast cereals, bread (white and brown)
- **Niacin:** liver, breakfast cereals, white bread, old potatoes, chicken
- **Vitamin C:** fruit juice, oranges, old potatoes, tomatoes
- **Vitamin D:** margarine, fatty fish, eggs, liver
- **Fibre:** dried beans, wholemeal bread, baked beans.

REMEMBER!

The extra costs needed for cooking and preparation.

Activity
a) Plan a week's basic shopping for a family of four – two adults (the father is unemployed) and two children, aged 5 and 7 (receiving free school meals).
  - Include staples such as bread, milk, margarine and the ingredients for three daily meals.
  - Ensure your basket will meet the nutritional needs of the family.
  - Include fresh fruit and vegetables.
  - Cost should include at least three main meat meals.
b) Assess the total spending.
c) Research the financial benefits a family like this would receive. Subtract the cost of your week' shopping and indicate how much would remain for other expenses.

Food allergies and intolerances

- An **allergy** is the body's rejection of a food.
- An **intolerance** is the body's inability to digest or absorb a specific food.

Many symptoms have been blamed on what is popularly, but inaccurately, called food allergy. Two in ten people in the population believe they are allergic to certain foods, but in reality less than 10 per cent of those can be proved medically. Only about 1 to 2 per cent of the population have proveable reactions to food, and only a minority of these reactions are true allergies. It is essential that accurate diagnosis is made before foods are withdrawn from a child's diet, because severe dietary modification can result in malnutrition. Frequently symptoms assumed to be related to food are in fact caused by a totally different trigger, such as an infection or stress.

FOODS PROVOKING ADVERSE REACTIONS

The most common foods which provoke reactions are milk, egg, fish and shellfish, nuts and peanuts, soya, pork, bacon, texturised meats, food additives, chocolate, coffee, tea, citrus fruit and strawberries,

SAFE PRACTICE

Always liaise with parents and carers so you know any foods that should not be given to a child.

WHAT IS AN ADVERSE REACTION TO FOOD?

An adverse reaction may simply be a result of dislike of a food, or it may be the result of a food allergy or of food poisoning.
- **Food dislike**
  - Psychological factors, for example the food may be associated with unpleasant feelings/occasions
  - Temporary intolerance – physical signs may include vomiting, diarrhoea, transient rashes
  - Food avoidance – tastes or textures may be unacceptable to the child, for example toddlers sometimes reject lumpy food for long periods.
- **Food allergy** – severe body response, including:
  - swelling of the mucous membranes leading to breathing difficulties
  - wheeziness
  - severe rashes
  - vomiting and diarrhoea
  - failure to thrive
  - symptoms worse when food eaten again
  - often not 'grown out of'.
- **Food poisoning** – the body's response to contaminated food, usually short-lived, but symptoms may be acute, including diarrhoea, vomiting and abdominal pain.

It is important to decide what is the cause of any adverse response to a certain meal or food.

In true allergy the symptoms are severe and can be life threatening. Such reactions may be caused by several factors, for example the lack of a particular enzyme needed for the digestion of food, or the presence of a toxin that irritates the lining of the intestine, or is itself toxic. Some foods, such as strawberries and shellfish, can release a histamine in susceptible children causing severe symptoms of rashes and wheeziness.

MILK PROTEIN ALLERGY

This is rare and can occur at any age. It is thought to affect about 2 per cent of children in the first year of life. It is is usually associated with a family history of allergy, for example asthma, hay fever or eczema. Treatment requires specialist advice. Soya milk and goat's milks have shown similar adverse responses to cow's milks and it is now advised that babies, following diagnosis, are fed a special milk formula made from hydrolysed protein and obtained on a prescription from a doctor,

LACTOSE INTOLERANCE

Lactose is the natural sugar found in milk and foods containing milk. Intolerance occurs when a baby lacks lactase, which is an enzyme needed to break down lactose into glucose for digestion. The baby will have diarrhoea, abdominal pain and frothy stools. Following diagnosis a special formula feed will be required. Children usually 'grow out' of this intolerance.

HYPERACTIVITY

Some children adopt abnormally active behaviour – they are restless, have poor concentration and need very little sleep. Occasionally this can be traced to a reaction to food or a food additive.

The prime causes are thought to be tartrazine, an orange colouring used in squashes and sweets, and benzoic acid, a preservative. Colourings used in foods are indicated on products as E numbers from 100–180, and preservatives with E numbers 200–283 (see Chapter 7).

Often other factors need to be taken into account before deciding that certain behaviour is caused by a food or an additive. The personality of the child, family tensions resulting from difficult or pre-term births, stressful childhood incidents, such as family breakdown, disruptions in routine and the 'normal' negativity of a 2-year-old, can all produce behaviour described as hyperactivity. Medical opinion is severely divided as to the true incidence of behaviour difficulties which are actually due to food additives. So, as with any other intolerance, careful diagnosis is essential before a severely restricting diet is applied to a young child.

Children often outgrow food intolerances and it is the usual practice for excluded foods to be reintroduced periodically under appropriate medical supervision. Certainly, no child should stay on a milk-free diet for longer than necessary. As well as the energy value of milk, calcium intake is important and can be affected.

TESTING FOR ALLERGIES AND INTOLERANCES

These tests should be undertaken by a medical team which include paediatricians and dieticians with specialist knowledge of the needs of growing children. A variety of tests can be undertaken. Exclusion of foods thought to provoke symptoms can be removed from the diet and then gradually reintroduced. These are most successful in 'double blind' trials, where children and their carers are given disguised foods so that psychological aversion (dislike) can be excluded and hidden clues are not inadvertently provided by the carer. Skins tests are not thought to be of great value and can be misused.

PREVENTION OF ALLERGY

All babies benefit from exclusive breast-feeding for the first four to six months of life, and breast-feeding should be encouraged in families with a history of allergies.

REMEMBER!

A true allergy can be life-threatening and you should always ensure that you know which children are at risk.

QUICK CHECK

1 Look at the following list. Do these outside influences affect children's nutrition in your placement?
   a) Is there a school 'tuck shop'?
   b) How near to the school gates can parents and carers or children buy sweets?
   c) Does the ice cream van regularly wait outside the playground?
   d) Is there a sweets policy in the school?
2 How could you provide interesting, balanced and varied diets from the 'cheap' source of nutrients listed on page 84?
3 What are the effects of poor diet on the total growth and development of a child?

4 What are the differences between:
   a) food dislike
   b) food allergy
   c) food poisoning?
5 Describe the symptoms of lactose intolerance.
6 What factors, other than the eating of specific food colourings, might cause a child to be labelled 'hyperactive'?
7 What nutritional advice regarding infant feeding, could you give an expectant mother with a family history of allergy and intolerance?
8 How may changes in government legislation have affected the nutritional content of school meals?
9 What suggestions could you make to a parent or carer about the safe packaging of packed lunches?
10 What is lactose intolerance?
11 Which additives/preservatives may be linked to hyperactivity in children?
12 Describe the life-threatening symptoms of true allergy?
13 List three cheap sources of high biological value (HBV) protein.
14 What are the social and emotional benefits of children eating school dinners?
15 Argue the case for packed lunches versus school dinners with a group of your peers.

KEY WORDS AND TERMS

You need to know what these words and phrases mean. Go back through the chapter and find out.

benefits
allergy
intolerance
milk protein allergy
lactose intolerance
hydrolysed protein

toxic
enzyme
'double blind' trial
hyperactivity
tartrazine

7 SAFE FOOD PREPARATION

> **This chapter covers:**
> - **Basic food hygiene**
> - **Food storage and processing**
> - **Food labelling and additives**

Basic food hygiene

When preparing and handling food for children, it is essential to maintain the highest standards of hygiene to prevent the spread of infections. Such infections are caused by harmful micro-organisms, known as pathogens, which contaminate (or spoil) the food when hygiene standards are not maintained.

CAUSES OF FOOD CONTAMINATION

The main causes of food contamination are bacteria, viruses, moulds and yeasts.

Bacteria
Bacteria are small, living organisms which are around us all the time. Most are harmless and some are even beneficial – those that live in our guts to digest foods, for example. However, some types of bacteria can affect flavours, cause food to smell, and even cause food poisoning.

Viruses
Viruses are tiny – smaller than bacteria. They only grow on living tissue and so cannot live in our food. They are less significant in contamination of food than bacteria, but can cause food-related illness, such as Hepatitis A, an infection of the liver causing jaundice and, less commonly, food poisoning.

Moulds
Moulds are tiny plants which form complex networks that we cannot see. They need oxygen to grow and because of this are usually seen only on the surface of foods. They can produce toxic substances that can penetrate foods.

Yeasts

Yeasts occur naturally on the surface of fruits and are also present in the air and soil. They multiply by 'budding' – producing buds which break off. Yeasts ferment sugars present in food to produce carbon dioxide and alcohol. This can be helpful, for example in the production of wines, but it can also cause spoilage of jams, etc.

Some contamination may be caused during food production. The use of chemicals, insecticides, etc. can affect our foods. As with viruses, these are much less likely to cause food poisoning than bacteria.

CONDITIONS FOR FOOD CONTAMINATION

For pathogens to thrive they need food, warmth, moisture and time.

Food

Bacteria, the most likely source of food poisoning, prefer certain foods to others. Cooked meats and meat products, gravies and stocks, milk, eggs and products made from them, shellfish and cooked rice all attract and encourage the growth of bacteria.

Some foods, however, have additives that inhibit bacterial growth. These include sugars, salt, preservatives and acids. Vacuum packaging, where oxygen has been removed, can also prevent deterioration. All of these limit bacteria multiplication to some extent.

Warmth

Blood heat is an ideal temperature for bacteria to grow. So temperatures higher than 63°C and lower than 5°C are fairly safe.

Most bacteria are killed by a constant temperature of at least 70°C that reaches to all the food. At temperatures of below 5°C (the correct temperature for refrigeration), bacteria do not grow and a few will die, but when food is returned to warm conditions multiplication will begin again.

SAFE PRACTICE

'Cool' spots from food reheated in a microwave can allow bacteria to breed. Reheated food must always be stirred and piping hot.

Moisture

Many of the high-risk foods contain moisture, which is essential for bacterial growth.

- Bacteria will multiply when fluids are added to reconstituted dried foods.
- The water in frozen foods (which is ice) is not available to the bacteria and provides safe storage, but only while the food is fully frozen.

Time

Bacteria grow by multiplication. In an ideal temperature they will grow by many thousands every four to five hours.

SAFE PRACTICE

Wipe and clear up crumbs and spills as you go.

CROSS CONTAMINATION

It is important to remember that poor personal hygiene and poor kitchen hygiene practices will add pathogens to, or contaminate, healthy food (see the charts below and on page 92).

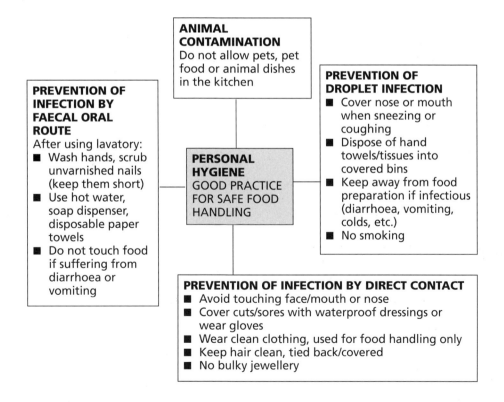

ANIMAL CONTAMINATION
Do not allow pets, pet food or animal dishes in the kitchen

PREVENTION OF INFECTION BY FAECAL ORAL ROUTE
After using lavatory:
- Wash hands, scrub unvarnished nails (keep them short)
- Use hot water, soap dispenser, disposable paper towels
- Do not touch food if suffering from diarrhoea or vomiting

PERSONAL HYGIENE
GOOD PRACTICE FOR SAFE FOOD HANDLING

PREVENTION OF DROPLET INFECTION
- Cover nose or mouth when sneezing or coughing
- Dispose of hand towels/tissues into covered bins
- Keep away from food preparation if infectious (diarrhoea, vomiting, colds, etc.)
- No smoking

PREVENTION OF INFECTION BY DIRECT CONTACT
- Avoid touching face/mouth or nose
- Cover cuts/sores with waterproof dressings or wear gloves
- Wear clean clothing, used for food handling only
- Keep hair clean, tied back/covered
- No bulky jewellery

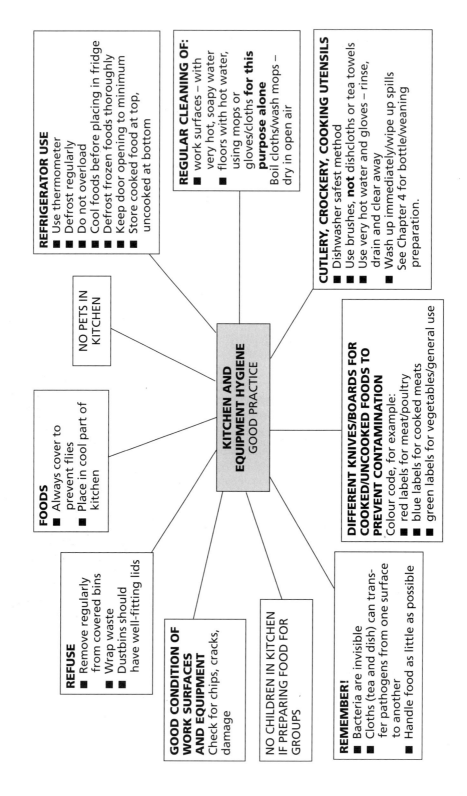

REFRIGERATOR USE
- Use thermometer
- Defrost regularly
- Do not overload
- Cool foods before placing in fridge
- Defrost frozen foods thoroughly
- Keep door opening to minimum
- Store cooked food at top, uncooked at bottom

REGULAR CLEANING OF:
- work surfaces – with very hot, soapy water
- floors with hot water, using mops or gloves/cloths **for this purpose alone**

Boil cloths/wash mops – dry in open air

CUTLERY, CROCKERY, COOKING UTENSILS
- Dishwasher safest method
- Use brushes, **not** dishcloths or tea towels
- Use very hot water and gloves – rinse, drain and clear away
- Wash up immediately/wipe up spills
- See Chapter 4 for bottle/weaning preparation.

NO PETS IN KITCHEN

FOODS
- Always cover to prevent flies
- Place in cool part of kitchen

KITCHEN AND EQUIPMENT HYGIENE
GOOD PRACTICE

DIFFERENT KNIVES/BOARDS FOR COOKED/UNCOOKED FOODS TO PREVENT CONTAMINATION
Colour code, for example:
- red labels for meat/poultry
- blue labels for cooked meats
- green labels for vegetables/general use

REFUSE
- Remove regularly from covered bins
- Wrap waste
- Dustbins should have well-fitting lids

GOOD CONDITION OF WORK SURFACES AND EQUIPMENT
Check for chips, cracks, damage

NO CHILDREN IN KITCHEN IF PREPARING FOOD FOR GROUPS

REMEMBER!
- Bacteria are invisible
- Cloths (tea and dish) can transfer pathogens from one surface to another
- Handle food as little as possible

Food storage and processing

HOW CAN WE GET THE BEST VALUE FROM OUR FOOD?

The nutritional content of any food will depend on:
- the composition of the raw food or ingredients as grown or bought
- the nutrients lost during storage, preparation or cooking and the addition of extra nutrients during manufacture
- how much is eaten
- the specific nutritional needs of the individual and whether these have already been met from other foods in the diet.

BUYING FOOD

Always buy from clean shops where assistants do not touch raw food with their bare hands, especially those foods that will not need to be cooked, such as cakes and cooked meats.

REMEMBER!

- Check that the shop is cool and that perishables are kept in a refridgerated display cabinet.
- Check that cooked and uncooked foods are kept separate.
- Check that foods are within their sell-by or best before dates.

COOKING AND PRESERVATION

Most foods have to be prepared and cooked before they can be eaten. At each stage some of the nutrients will be lost or reduced. Further nutrients may be lost if the food is stored for long periods in conditions that are not ideal.

The aim is to keep these losses to a minimum, and fresh foods should be eaten wherever possible.

Home cooking

Heat is generally applied to food in one of three ways:
- directly, with or without additional fat – roasting, grilling, baking and microwave cooking
- with water – boiling, stewing and braising
- with fat – frying.

Heat causes chemical and physical changes in food which in general improve flavour, palatability and digestibility. Heat may also increase the availability of some nutrients by destroying enzymes and anti-digestive factors. However, cooking more usually results in the loss of nutrients.

Aim to grill rather than fry foods. Grilling allows fat from foods to pass into the grill pan rather than being retained within the food.

Microwave cooking is quick with little nutrient loss. However, care needs to be taken to ensure previously cooked food is thoroughly re-heated and piping hot.

Chopping foods such as fruit and vegetables a long time before cooking causes considerable vitamin loss. Try to prepare such foods just before cooking and plunge them into already boiling water. This will help reduce the loss of vitamins B and C.

REMEMBER!

The greatest nutrient losses are with:
- high temperatures
- long cooking times
- large amounts of liquid.

Activity

Bearing in mind that vitamins B and C are lost into the cooking water when vegetables are cooked, how might these nutrients still be 'saved' and used in a child's meal?

PRESERVATION METHODS

Home freezing

This may result in some loss of thiamin and vitamin C when vegetables are blanched in water before freezing, but less than would otherwise happen in storage. If the temperature of the freezer is kept below −18°C there is almost no further loss of nutritional value until the food is thawed. In general, differences between the nutrient content of cooked fresh foods and cooked frozen foods are small.

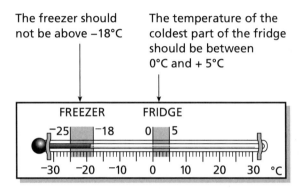

Temperatures for home storage in the fridge or freezer

Industrial processing

As with home freezing, the process itself has little effect on nutritional value and since the delay between harvesting and processing is minimal, the nutrients in the high quality fresh foods that are used are generally well retained.

Canning and bottling

The heat used in this process will reduce the amounts of heat sensitive vitamins, especially thiamin, folic acid and vitamin C. The losses will depend on the length of time needed to destroy pathogens and to cook the food. They will be greater for larger cans and in foods of close consistency, such as ham, because of the slow transfer of heat from the outside to the centre.

Dehydration

In carefully controlled conditions this has little effect on most nutrients, but about half the vitamin C is lost. Suitable packaging is important to limit further loss during long storage.

Irradiation

In this process, food is exposed under controlled conditions to gamma rays from a radioactive source. But the food is not left radioactive.

The process is used to slow down the ripening process of fruits and vegetables, extend the shelf-life of many foods, reducing storage problems and to sterilise some products, such as chicken. It cannot be used on dairy products and oily fish because it alters their taste. It is thought that small losses of vitamin C, thiamin, vitamin E and some fatty acids can occur, but the amounts are variable and dependant upon the dosages used.

Food labelling and additives

Food labels should tell us about the contents of a tin or packet, but they can be very confusing.

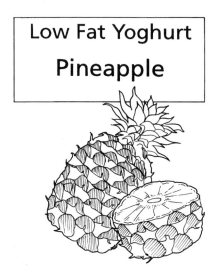

Low Fat Yoghurt

Pineapple

DISPLAY UNTIL	USE BY
06OCT	08OCT
KEEP REFRIGERATED DO NOT FREEZE	

NUTRITION

TYPICAL COMPOSITION	Each Pot (150g) provides	100g (3½oz) provide
Energy	608kJ/145kcal	405kJ/97kcal
Protein	8.6g	5.7g
Carbohydrate	25.8g	17.2g
of which sugars	25.8g	17.2g
Fat	1.4g	0.9g
of which saturates	0.8g	0.5g
polyunsaturates	0.2g	0.1g
Sodium	0.1g	0.1g
VITAMINS/ MINERALS	%RECOMMENDED DAILY AMOUNT	
Calcium	61	

INFORMATION

ADDED INGREDIENTS: SUGAR, PINEAPPLE, PINEAPPLE PUREE, STABILISERS (PECTIN, CAROB GUM), FLAVOURINGS

150 g e

SUITABLE FOR
VEGETARIANS

Activity
The label above tells you:
- name and description of the food
- ingredients and energy content
- composition, per pot and per 100 g

The main points to look for on food labels are:

■ the name or description of the food – by law this has to be clear and informative. A trade mark or brand name is not allowed as a substitute for a clear name and description of the food.
■ where the food is made
■ how long and under what conditions the food can be kept – the 'best before' and 'use by' information. This is not necessary for all foods, for example sugar and sugar-based foods, fresh fruit and vegetables are exempt from this requirement. The label will also give any instructions as to correct storage, for example in a cool dark cupboard or in a refrigerator.
■ weight, volume or number in the pack
■ place of origin
■ preparation or cooking instructions
■ name and address of the manufacturer.

In addition, many labels now include nutritional information. Labels on most pre-packed foods must include a complete list of ingredients. Although the actual quantities are not normally given, the ingredients must be listed in descending order of weight – the first ingredient in the list will be the one that weighed the most when it went into the food. The presence of water, unless only a tiny amount, must also be indicated.

Health claims made about foods are not allowed. Regulations covering medicines are strict and food is not covered by such control. So claims of prevention or cures of illness or disease by a 'health' food are not allowed

ADDITIVES

The list of ingredients must also show any **additives** that have been used in the food. Most approved additives have an indentifying number – a simple coding system introduced to avoid long chemical names on labels. If the additive has been approved by the European Union as well as by the United Kingdom there is an 'E' in front of the number. Usually a category name such as 'preservative' must come before the additive number to tell you why it has been included, for example Preservative E200.

Flavourings which are used in very small amounts are not currently controlled in this way although, like other additives, they can only be used in food if they are safe. Labels must state that flavourings have been used but need not list them.

Why are additives included?

Additives have several functions – as preservatives, colourings, flavour enhancers, emulsifiers and antioxidants (see below). They may be natural (sugar, salt, garlic, herbs) or artificial. Artificial additives may be modified natural substances or manufactured. They are identified by E numbers on food labels. Some children may develop allergies to an additive (see Chapter 6, page 86).

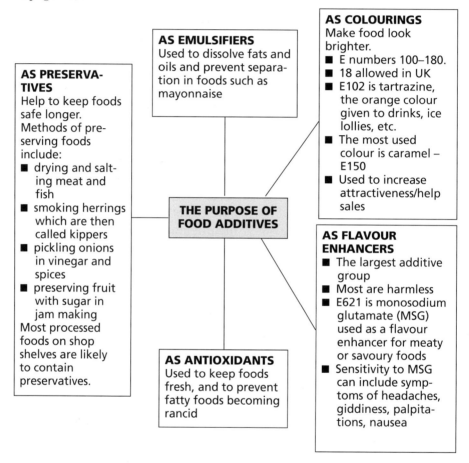

AS PRESERVATIVES
Help to keep foods safe longer.
Methods of preserving foods include:
■ drying and salting meat and fish
■ smoking herrings which are then called kippers
■ pickling onions in vinegar and spices
■ preserving fruit with sugar in jam making
Most processed foods on shop shelves are likely to contain preservatives.

AS EMULSIFIERS
Used to dissolve fats and oils and prevent separation in foods such as mayonnaise

AS COLOURINGS
Make food look brighter.
■ E numbers 100–180.
■ 18 allowed in UK
■ E102 is tartrazine, the orange colour given to drinks, ice lollies, etc.
■ The most used colour is caramel – E150
■ Used to increase attractiveness/help sales

THE PURPOSE OF FOOD ADDITIVES

AS FLAVOUR ENHANCERS
■ The largest additive group
■ Most are harmless
■ E621 is monosodium glutamate (MSG) used as a flavour enhancer for meaty or savoury foods
■ Sensitivity to MSG can include symptoms of headaches, giddiness, palpitations, nausea

AS ANTIOXIDANTS
Used to keep foods fresh, and to prevent fatty foods becoming rancid

Activity

Visit a local supermarket and look at the food labels on branded goods.

a) Is the information easily understood? Would it help you in meal planning?

b) Is there additional nutritional information provided by the particular supermarket? Would this be useful for you?

c) Do you consider that particular foods are given 'healthy' claims by this information? Do you consider this justified?

QUICK CHECK

1 What are bacteria and what effect can they have on food?
2 Describe the ideal conditions for pathogens to multiply when handling or preparing food.
3 How can yeasts affect foods?
4 List the foods which are most likely to be the source of food poisoning?
5 What is the safe temperature for a refrigerator?
6 Describe how you use a refrigerator to maintain a correct temperature.
7 Explain the term 'cross contamination'.
8 List the personal hygiene measures essential for safe food handling.
9 What is the safest and most effective way of washing up?
10 What are the differences in calorific value between a boiled chicken and a roasted chicken?
11 Which preservation methods best retain water-soluble vitamins?
12 How can you tell if a food additive has been approved by the European Union?
13 What are the main reasons for including the following in food:
   a) preservatives?
   b) additives?
14 What is the difference between:
   a) an emulsifier, and
   b) an antioxidant?
15 Which is the most effective method of preserving water-soluble vitamins, bottling or freezing?

KEY WORDS AND TERMS

You need to know what these words and phrases mean. Go back through the chapter and find out.

moulds	dehydration
yeasts	irradiation
preservatives	E numbers
additives	toxins
industrial processing	pathogens

8 SPECIAL DIETS AND NUTRITIONAL DISORDERS

> **This chapter covers:**
> - Special diets
> - Nutritional disorders:
>   - Overweight and obesity
>   - Dental caries
>   - Iron deficiency anaemia
>   - Constipation
>   - Diarrhoea and vomiting
>   - Vitamin deficiency disorders
>   - Coeliac disease
>   - Cystic fibrosis
>   - Phenylketonuria
>   - Diabetes mellitus
>   - Failure to thrive

Whenever essential nutrients are missing from a child's diet, either because the diet is poor or because the nutrients cannot be absorbed or used by the child's body, that child's growth, health and development are going to be affected in some way. Obviously, the effects on the child will depend on which nutrients are missing but, typically, there may be:
- poor growth (weight, height and head circumference)
- delayed learning and physical development
- recurrent health problems, such as coughs and colds, chest infections and anaemia
- social and emotional problems.

Children with nutritional disorders may spend time in hospital separated from family, friends and peers, perhaps undergoing unpleasant tests and treatment and possibly missing valuable time at nursery and school. Some disorders are preventable by making sure children receive balanced and wholesome diets. Others, due to allergies, intolerances and other medical conditions, can be alleviated by modern treatment and expert dietary advice so that, as far as possible, normal growth and development take place.

Excessive intake of calories leads to obesity, the most common form of over-nutrition in well-off countries. Too many sugary foods and drinks will cause dental caries.

Special diets

Special diets are worked out by the doctor and dietician according to the individual needs of the child. The diet may need adjusting from time to time especially when nutritional needs alter as the child grows. Cultural and religious dietary traditions will be taken into account when planning a diet. The hospital or community dietician will supervise the diet and provide help and advice for the parents and carers.

Nurseries and schools need to know of, and record, any special medical diet and medicines a child may be receiving. This involves close liaison and co-operation between nursery or school staff and her parents and carers. Supervision of the child at meal times should ensure that her diet foods are not swapped with her friends' foods. A child who has to maintain a restricting life-long diet for health reasons will need considerable support during her nursery or school day. A young child, particularly, will need simple and consistent explanations as to why certain foods are not allowed. As she gets older, she will become expert at what is or is not permitted and generally she will adapt and manage easily, making the link betwen feeling healthy and keeping to her diet.

Difficulties can occur with parties, visits and outings. Liaison with parents and carers at such times will be valuable. Many diets must be eaten at regular times in order to maintain good health. This may cause problems if a toddler decides to assert her independence and refuses to eat or uses food as a power tool.

Professionals such as the health visitor and nursery nurse can offer support, encouragement and practical help to parents and carers. Voluntary and self-help organisations offer ready advice. Team work, understanding and up-to-date knowledge of the long-term implications of failure to keep to the diet will be necessary. The paediatrician and family doctor will regularly assess the child's health and development.

Activity

Research the following questions and write up your findings.
a) Is there a child in your nursery or school who must follow a special diet?
b) What are the reasons for the diet and which foods are restricted?
c) Where is the record of the diet kept?
d) Are meal timings important?

Nutritional disorders

OVERWEIGHT AND OBESITY

- Overweight = 10–20 per cent over ideal weight.
- Obesity = 20 per cent (or more) over ideal weight.

The most common cause is excess calorie intake over energy expenditure. In other words, more food is eaten than the body needs and the excess is stored as fat. It is common in childhood and there is often a family pattern of overweight. Disabilities which restrict physical activity and some hormonal disorders lead to obesity in a few children.

Health education and dietary guidelines for health professionals and parents/carers plus a greater awareness of overweight and obesity and its effect on child health can help to reduce its incidence.

Overweight and obesity in infancy

An overfed baby will develop extra fat cells which then continuously demand to be filled. The effects of this may include:

- delayed motor development (rolling, crawling, walking, climbing, running)
- mechanical disorders of hips, legs and feet
- greater risk of accidents
- recurrent chest infections
- chafing and soreness where skin surfaces rub together
- breathlessness
- greater expectations by adults because baby looks older.

Possible causes are:
- over-concentrated bottle feeds; encouraging baby to finish up bottle when she is clearly satisfied
- addition of sugar and/or cereal to bottle feed
- early introduction of weaning foods
- insisting baby 'eats everything up'
- too many snacks
- lack of opportunity and encouragement for physical activity – long periods of time spent in cot, pram, bouncing chair or playpen

Prevention and management

The aim is to slow down the rate of weight gain or temporarily halt it. A *slow* weight loss may be desirable in the older baby (9–12 months) if there is marked obesity, but remember that babies need a nutritious diet at all times.

Practical measures include:

- encouraging mothers to breast feed
- making up bottle feeds correctly – no added sugar or solids
- avoidance of early weaning (not before 4 months) – see Chapter 4, pages 60–1
- allowing the baby's appetite to dictate how much food is eaten – encourage finger foods and self-feeding
- providing opportunity and encouragement for physical activity
- liaison between nursery staff and parent/carer:
  - keep a record of food and drink intake
  - the amount of milk should not exceed 1 pint a day as solid food increases
  - avoid offering sugary foods and drinks.
- regular growth checks – record the measurements on the baby's percentile (growth) chart (see page 118).

Overweight and obesity in childhood

The effects may include:

- appearance – the child looks fat (plump abdomen, thighs and upper arms; when standing straight the ankles, knees and thighs are touching). Knock-knees are common and there may be back and posture problems
- measurements of the skin folds around the upper arms, just below the waist and below the shoulder blades will be above normal
- above 'ideal' weight and height measurements – a child may be taller than expected due to increased protein intake
- difficulty with gross motor skills – PE, games and sports
- embarrassment at having to change for games and swimming
- being teased and called 'fatty', leading to poor self-image and possible school refusal
- social isolation
- difficulty in buying/choosing clothes – clothes often several sizes bigger than recommended age-size.

Possible causes are:

- a pattern of eating large meals
- snacking and grazing on high calorie foods
- lack of physical exercise
- economical and psychological factors (see Chapter 5, page 74).

Prevention and management

During infancy and early childhood parents and carers have the ideal opportunity to promote healthy eating habits and exercise control over what children eat. Sensible eating from the five food groups and daily exercise is the best prevention and can be undertaken by all family members. Any diet plan for an overweight or obese child will aim to prevent further weight gain or encourage a *gradual* loss. Parents' and carers' co-operation and involvement is important. Nursery and school staff will be able to help them in supporting and encouraging the child.

The diet should include:

- adequate protein, vitamin and mineral intake provided by lean meat, fish, milk, cheese, eggs, fresh fruit and vegetables
- reduction of calorie intake, especially fatty and 'empty calorie' foods
- not more than 1 pint of milk a day – semi-skimmed milk may be recommended if the child is over 2 years
- three appealing, nutritious meals a day, plus two or three healthy snacks of fresh fruit or vegetables
- vitamin supplements should be continued.

In addition:

- adequate opportunity should be provided for indoor and outdoor physical activity for all age groups
- encourage independence in skills such as feeding, dressing, and undressing
- monitor time spent watching television and playing computer games
- growth should be measured and recorded at regular intervals
- rewards for progress may be given, for example a special outing or a new item of clothing.

REMEMBER!

It is important that a child knows why her diet is resticted. The diet will fail if the child is not informed, involved and co-operative.

Adulthood

Overweight children may become overweight adults with health risks of:

- coronary heart disease
- raised blood pressure
- chest infections
- varicose veins
- arthritis
- postural problems
- possible infertility
- greater risk of accidents and toxaemia of pregnancy
- shorter life expectancy.

DENTAL CARIES

Dental caries (tooth decay) is an extremely common problem among young children. It leads to pain, fillings and extractions. It is not uncommon to see pre-school children with several filled teeth and gaps where teeth have been extracted. The diagram below shows the progress of tooth decay.

HOW TOOTH DECAY OCCURS

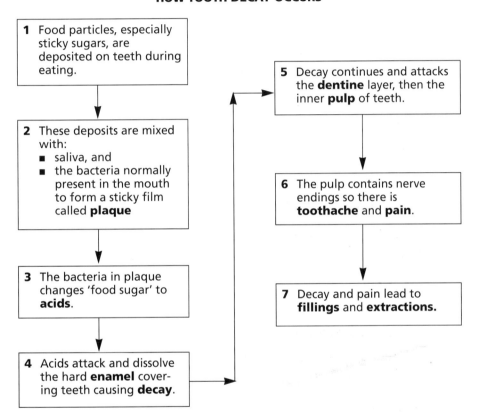

Sugary foods and drinks are the main cause of tooth decay. The longer sugars remain in the mouth, the greater the damage will be. Children who do not eat sweets and sugary foods or drink sweet drinks are less likely to need fillings and extractions. Tooth extractions in the years before natural loss of deciduous (milk) teeth can lead to gum shrinkage as well as eating, speech and emotional problems. However, it is unrealistic to ban sweets and sugary foods and drinks altogether. If you understand the relationship between eating sugars and tooth decay you can help parents and carers to care for their children's teeth.

All carers can easily follow these helpful rules:

- Dummies dipped in sugar or honey and bottles of sugar water or sweet fruit drink should not be given as comforters. Check labels on herbal and fruit drinks – they may say 'no added sweetening' but may be high in natural sugar and should be well-diluted before giving them to a baby or young child. Cooled, boiled water should be offered in preference to fruit drinks. Weaning foods should be as sugar-free as possible. Foods which encourage a baby to chew can be offered from around 7 months.
- Offer children a well-balanced diet. Include hard, raw fruit and vegetables (apples, carrots, celery) and wholegrain foods all of which encourage chewing. Chewing increases the blood supply to the teeth, gums and jaws aiding their healthy growth and development and helping normal speech. It also increases the flow of saliva which helps to keep the teeth clean.
- Sweets, biscuits, fizzy drinks, etc., should be discouraged especially if they are going to be eaten or drunk over a period of time. Sweets, if given, are best offered at a specific time (perhaps after a meal) followed by thorough teeth cleaning.

REMEMBER!

Eating and drinking sugary food and drinks automatically increases acid production in the mouth.

- Start dental care as soon as the first tooth appears. Wipe over the tooth and gums with a clean, non-fluffy cloth or use a small toothbrush and a tiny amount of toothpaste. Young children should clean their teeth in the morning and last thing at night as well as after meals and after eating sweets. In many nurseries, children have the opportunity to clean their teeth after meals.

REMEMBER!

Cleaning teeth is a difficult task to perform correctly, especially the inner aspect of the back teeth, and young children need help and supervision.

- The mineral fluoride guards against tooth decay by protecting the enamel from acid attack. It is found naturally in the drinking water in some areas, while in others it has been added. Where there is no fluoridation of water, fluoride drops or tablets may be prescribed. Too much fluoride can cause softening of the teeth as well as brown staining, white mottling and delayed shedding. Many toothpastes now contain fluoride but only small amounts should be used.

■ Regular dental check-ups, starting in the second year, are recommended. The dentist will advise on fluoride treatment and the correct technique for cleaning teeth.

REMEMBER!

Dental caries is preventable by appropriate diet, regular and correct cleaning of teeth and regular dental inspections.

Activity
a) Ask the children in your placement how often they eat sweets – every day? once a week? never?
b) Ask them how frequently they clean their teeth and, if they are able to tell you, when they last visited the dentist.
c) Collate your information and set it out as a pie chart or histogram. Your college tutor will help you with this.

IRON DEFICIENCY ANAEMIA

This is the most common form of anaemia. Lack of iron prevents the production of haemoglobin, a protein in red blood cells which transports oxygen around the body.

Sufficient iron is stored in a baby's liver for the first four months of life. Babies who are born pre-term do not have these stores of iron and are at risk of anaemia especially during the first year. A poor diet at any age can cause anaemia, but toddlers who may be reluctant to eat solids are particularly vulnerable. It is also common in coeliac disease (see page 110) because of poor iron absorption.

Recognising anaemia in children

A child with anaemia is likely to look pale. The mucous membranes inside the eyelids and mouth will also be pale – possibly the only noticeable areas of pallor in a child with black skin. You may notice that she tires quickly, lacks energy and is breathless during physical activity. Other signs can include poor appetite, irritability, frequent infections and delayed growth. Nausea, vomiting and fainting may occur. A low haemoglobin level in a blood test indicates anaemia.

Treatment and prevention of anaemia

Treatment
Iron-rich foods plus iron supplements in the form of medicine or tablets are the mainstay of treatment. Because appetite is poor, it may be difficult to get a young child to eat iron-rich foods.

■ The best dietary iron is contained in foods such as red meat, liver and meat products. It is called haem-iron and is readily absorbed by the body. Many children do not like liver on its own, but it can be finely chopped and added to casseroles and mince dishes.

■ Non-haem iron, present in plant and vegetable foods such as pulses, cereals, green leafy vegetables, dried fruit and cocoa, is less well absorbed and it is important that adequate vitamin C, which assists absorption of iron, is provided with these foods. For example: a portion of Weetabix and a diluted pure orange juice drink, lentil lasagne and fresh fruit salad, vegetarian quiche and green salad with tomatoes. Offer breakfast cereals which are fortified with iron.

■ Iron medicine tends to discolour teeth so it is best taken through a straw. Regular brushing of teeth is important. Never put iron medicine in food. Older children may be able to take iron tablets. Iron supplements will turn the stools black. Always make a written record of any medicine or tablets given to a child in the nursery or school.

Repeat blood tests will be necessary.

Prevention
Encourage regular and healthy meals and snacks by offering a variety of foods from the food groups. Discourage 'snacking' on high calorie foods which leave little room for essential nutritious foods.

Activity
Find out about and write up the following information:
a) Which medicines, if any, are parents/carers allowed to bring into nursery or school for their children?
b) Where are medicines stored?
c) What is the procedure for giving medicines and what details are recorded?

CONSTIPATION

Constipation is the passing of hard, infrequent and possibly painful stools. The longer faeces remain in the lower bowel the greater the risk of constipation. It is a common problem in young children and creates misery for them and their parents. A situation may develop in which a child is frightened to pass a stool and the longer she delays the greater the discomfort and difficulty. Sometimes straining to pass a hard stool causes an anal fissure – a small crack in the mucous membrane of the anus – with some spotting of blood. This causes further pain.

Possible causes include:
■ poor diet with insufficient fibre and fluid intake
■ illness or operation when a child's food intake has been reduced
■ mismanagement of toilet training and over-emphasis on bowel function
■ emotional problems leading to 'stool holding'.

Prevention of constipation
Make sure children's diets contain sufficient fibre in the form of wholegrain foods, fresh fruit and vegetables. Fibre keeps the faeces bulky, because it is not digested, and soft, because it absorbs water in the large intestine. Bulky, soft faeces are easy to pass. Have drinks of water available for children during the day. Diluted fresh orange juice or prune juice may be helpful. Laxatives should not be given without medical approval. Emotional causes of constipation may be more difficult to resolve and need specialist help. Management of toilet training is covered widely in other textbooks.

DIARRHOEA AND VOMITING

Diarrhoea (frequent loose, watery stools) and vomiting can occur separately or together. For diarrhoea to occur, something (often infection) causes quickened peristalsis and the rapid movement of food and drink through the intestines before absorption of nutrients and water can take place.

The cause of vomiting may not always be immediately obvious but must never be ignored. Always seek medical advice urgently for a baby with a combination of diarrhoea and vomiting or if baby appears unwell with either diarrhoea or vomiting. Dehydration can occur quickly, with loss of essential minerals from the body as well as weight loss. With an older child it may be all right to wait 24 hours to see if there is improvement unless the child is obviously unwell.

Water (cool, boiled for babies) or well-diluted fruit juice can be offered. The doctor may advise oral rehydration solutions (glucose and salt) such as Dioralyte or Rehidrat.

'Toddler diarrhoea' is a recognised condition in which diarrhoea occurs for several days at a time. The stools contain undigested food. The child appears well and active and there is usually no cause for concern although a check-up with the doctor is advisable. As the toddler gets older the diarrhoea ceases.

VITAMIN DEFICIENCY DISORDERS

These occur either from a lack of a particular vitamin in the diet or as a result of failure of absorption due to an intestinal problem. Breast milk will contain all the vitamins a baby needs as long as the mother's diet is balanced and varied. Formula milks are fortified with vitamins.

Although vitamin deficiencies are relatively uncommon, the rapid growth and development taking place in infancy and childhood makes deficiency a possibility, and rickets and scurvy are still seen in children.

Rickets is more commonly seen among the Asian population. This is due to a lack of vitamin D in their traditional cereal and vegetable diet as well as dress customs which may result in less exposure to sunlight. Margarine, eggs and oily fish (all sources of vitamin D) can be included in the diet. Daily vitamin A, D and C supplements from the onset of weaning up to 5 years will ensure adequate vitamin intake for all children especially those who may be receiving poor diets or going through a fussy stage of eating. Vitamin drops should not be put in a baby's bottle – she may not finish her feed, and also the drops will stick to the side of the bottle.

The times of greatest risk of vitamin deficiency are:
- during weaning when feeding moves from a milk diet to solid foods
- during the toddler stage when food fads are common
- during illness
- in restricted diets, such as vegan and macrobiotic diets, and in cases of food allergy or intolerance.

Infants need large amounts of calcium because of their fast growth rate and vitamin D is needed for calcium absorption. Because sunshine is the best source of vitamin D, they are particularly at risk of deficiency if kept indoors for long periods, covered up too much when outdoors or when sunshine is scarce.

Table 8.1 lists the main vitamin deficiency disorders.

COELIAC DISEASE

Coeliac disease (gluten intolerance) is nearly always detected in infancy or childhood and it often occurs in families. It is caused by intolerance to gluten, the protein found in wheat, barley, rye and oats. Gluten damages the lining of the intestine resulting in poor absorption of essential nutrients. Symptoms usually start within a few months of gluten foods being introduced during the weaning process. The first signs are usually loose, bulky, greasy, smelly stools (steatorrhoea) which are difficult to flush away. Failure to thrive, developmental delay, lethargy, irritability and lack of enthusiasm are typically seen. There is also muscle wasting, especially of the buttocks, and a distended stomach (see page 113).

Table 8.1 Vitamin deficiency disorders

Vitamin	Disorder	Signs and symptoms of deficiency	Treatment	Notes
Vitamin A	1 Night blindness 2 Skin and respiratory problems 3 Xerophthalmia leading to blindness	1 Inability to see in dim light 2 ■ Dry, scaly roughened skin ■ Itchy skin and eyes ■ Respiratory tract infections 3 Softening of cornea and eye infections causing permanent eye damage	■ Large doses vitamin A ■ Diet rich in dairy foods and fish liver oils ■ Dark green, yellow and orange vegetables and fruit	Vitamin supplements and fortified margarine make deficiency rare, although it still occurs in India and Africa where many children become blind
Vitamin B_1	Beri-beri	■ Listlessness and irritability ■ Poor appetite ■ Vomiting and constipation ■ Nerve damage leading to pain in legs and feet ■ Heart enlargement The onset may be acute in infants causing heart problems	■ Vitamin B_1 supplement ■ Diet rich in thiamin – pulses, egg yolk, liver, fortified cereals	Occurs mainly in countries where polished (white) rice is the staple food. Polishing/refining the rice removes the husk containing vitamin B_1
Folic acid/folate	1 Anaemia 2 Neural tube defects	1 See page 107 2 Spina bifida and anencephaly (abnormalities of the spinal cord and brain) are linked to folic acid deficiency	1 Management of anaemia (see page 107) and folic acid supplements 2 Management and treatment according to baby's needs	■ Iron and folic acid supplements recommended pre-conceptually and in early pregnancy plus diet rich in wholegrains, meat, dark leafy vegetables, carrots, milk ■ Malabsorption of folic acid often occurs in coeliac disease

(continued)

Table 8.1 Vitamin deficiency disorders (*continued*)

Vitamin	Disorder	Signs and symptoms of deficiency	Treatment	Notes
Niacin	Pellagra	■ Loss of weight ■ Rough, thickened skin with reddish/brown areas appearing on face, neck and hands ■ Irritability ■ Diarrhoea ■ Mental confusion	■ Niacin supplements ■ Bread and maize fortified with niacin	Mostly seen in Africa and India where maize, a poor source of niacin, is a staple food
Vitamin C	Scurvy	■ Swollen, bleeding gums ■ Tendency to bruise easily ■ Painful, tender limbs ■ Poor resistance to infection ■ Anaemia	■ Vitamin C supplements ■ Fresh citrus fruits ■ Fresh vegetables	■ Vitamin C easily lost in cooking and exposure to air ■ Pain is quickly relieved once treatment is started
Vitamin D	Rickets	■ Delayed closure of anterior fontanelle ■ Soft deformed bones ■ Painful joints ■ Postural deformities – bow legs, curvature of spine ■ Poor muscle tone ■ Delayed motor development and dentition ■ 'Rickety rosary' – prominent beads of cartilage down sides of ribs	■ Large doses vitamin D ■ At least 1 pint milk daily for calcium content ■ No weight bearing until bones and joints are healing	■ Children who receive little exposure to sunlight may be at risk of deficiency ■ Diets in which cereals and vegetables are staple foods are likely to be deficient in vitamin D

Coeliac disease is permanent, but the child will thrive and remain well and healthy with a gluten-free diet. If the diet lapses the symptoms will reappear. Additional vitamin D, iron and folic acid are usually prescribed.

Gluten-free weaning foods and other products are identified by the crossed grain symbol or the words 'gluten-free' on the packaging. Some are available on prescription. Always check the labels of foods you are not sure of and encourage parents and carers to do the same. Many manufactured baby foods, processed meat products and soups contain 'hidden' gluten. Flours, breads, cakes and biscuits can be made from grains such as rice, corn, maize and millet as well as from potatoes, soya bean and chick peas. Milk and dairy foods, fresh meat, fish, fruit and fresh vegetables can be eaten. Offering gluten-free weaning cereals, such as rice and maize, to all infants under 6 months reduces the risk of coeliac disease.

The Coeliac Society produces a list of gluten-free manufactured products.

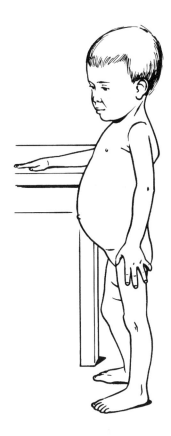

A child with coeliac disease. Note the distended abdomen and wasted buttocks

The crossed grain symbol which indicates that food is gluten-free

Activity
a) Obtain a current copy of the Coeliac Society's list of gluten-free products (see page 145 for the address).
b) Visit a supermarket and see how many of the listed foods you can find.
c) How time-consuming was this exercise?

CYSTIC FIBROSIS

Cystic fibrosis is genetically inherited and affects 1 to 2 children per 2000 births. Many children with cystic fibrosis used to die in childhood or their early teens but, with better knowledge of the disease and advances in treatment, they are now surviving well into adulthood. Heart and lung transplants are offering a cure to some sufferers.

Symptoms, which occur within the first few months of life, affect the lungs and the digestive system. Large quantities of thick, sticky mucus form in the airways and the ducts of the pancreas. Lung problems include coughs, colds, recurrent chest infections and lung damage. Blockage of the pancreatic ducts means that many of the enzymes needed to digest and absorb food cannot pass into the intestines.

Despite having a good appetite, a child with cystic fibrosis will fail to grow or gain weight. The stools are bulky, pale and foul smelling and contain large quantities of undigested protein and fats. When the child's sweat is examined it contains an abnormally high sodium level – a typical sign of cystic fibrosis.

Care and treatment

Diet
A high calorie and protein diet is needed but with a decreased intake of fat. Multi-vitamin supplements are given. Salt intake may be increased in hot weather or during excessive activity as sweating is increased.

Medicines
A pancreatic enzyme is taken with meals to aid absorption of nutrients. Antibiotics are often prescribed on a long-term basis to prevent chest infections.

Physiotherapy and physical exercise
Physiotherapy is carried out several times a day to help the child cough up mucus and keep the lungs clear and working properly. Outdoor physical activity, swimming and PE, music and movement (all typically provided in nursery and school) are ideal exercises for a child with cystic fibrosis.

PHENYLKETONURIA

Phenylketonuria (PKU) is genetically inherited and occurs in about 1 in 10 000 births. It is caused by excess of phenylalanine, an essential amino acid, which cannot be broken down and absorbed by the body due to the lack of a liver enzyme. It builds up in the blood stream and causes brain damage and learning delay. There is no cure but early diagnosis and treatment will promote normal development and learning.

All newborn babies are screened (the Guthrie Test) for this disorder between six to twelve days after birth, by which time the baby has had several days of milk feeds. The Guthrie Test involves testing a sample of blood from a heel prick for the level of phenylalanine. An abnormally high level confirms the diagnosis. Treatment is dietary and life-long. The main aspects of the diet, which must provide adequate protein for growth, are:

- special infant formula feed (a small feed of breast milk may be given *after* the formula feed)
- small amounts of natural protein plus substitute protein formula foods which are available on prescription
- vitamin and mineral supplements taken with the protein substitute or as a medicine.

A woman with phenylketonuria needs to maintain a low-phenylalanine diet during pregnancy to reduce the risk of harm to her baby

Babies and young children with phenylketonuria will have regular blood tests. Normal learning can be achieved by keeping to the diet which is one of the most restrictive of all special diets. It may be possible to relax some dietary rules once brain growth is complete. As a general rule, high protein foods such as meat, fish, cheese, eggs and pulses may not be eaten. Milk, cereals and potatoes may be allowed in small amounts. Fruit and most vegetables, fats, sugars, and special breads and pasta are allowed.

DIABETES MELLITUS

Diabetes mellitus is a hormonal disorder affecting carbohydrate metabolism. It is rare under 2 years of age. Normally, the hormone insulin, produced by the pancreas, breaks down sugar (glucose) in the blood and converts it into energy for use by the body. In diabetes there is little or no insulin produced for this conversion and the blood sugar level rises spilling over into the urine. The child passes large amounts of urine and becomes excessively thirsty. Bedwetting may occur.

With little energy available from sugar, the body breaks down fat and protein leading to weight loss, hunger and increased appetite. The breakdown of fats produces ketones which smell like pear drops on the child's breath and may also be present in the urine. At this stage the child may be very ill.

Care and treatment

There is no cure for diabetes but on-going medical care and special diet means that the child can lead a normal life. Daily insulin injections will keep the blood sugar level as normal as possible – insulin cannot be given by mouth because it is protein-based and would be digested before it could take effect. More insulin may be needed at times of increased activity or during illness.

The diet will be well-balanced, matching carbohydrate intake to the amounts of insulin prescribed. It may take a little time to adjust this. The child will need to eat specified amounts at regular times. Food lists provided by the dietician will offer a range of foods which means a varied diet is possible. Failure to keep to the diet may result in long-term problems especially of the eyes and circulatory system.

Nursery and school staff need to know the signs of hypoglycaemia and hyperglycaemia (see page 117) and a ready supply of easily absorbed sugar such as a sugary drink (carton of orange juice), sugar lumps or glucose tablets should be available. Children with diabetes must carry such sugar supplies with them as well as some form of identification (a bracelet or pendant). A child with diabetes should never be kept waiting for, or miss, a meal.

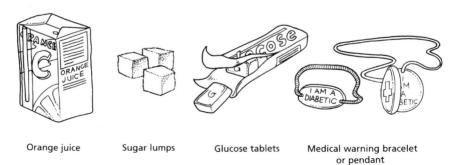

| Orange juice | Sugar lumps | Glucose tablets | Medical warning bracelet or pendant |

Essential items for a child with diabetes

Hypoglycaemia

Hypoglycaemia ('a hypo') occurs when the blood sugar level is too low. It occurs suddenly.

It is caused by too little food, too much insulin or excessive exercise without adequate food intake. Signs inclue dizziness, loss of concentration, vagueness, sweating, pallor, sickness. Care of child: give sugary drink or lump of sugar. Get medical help quickly if the child loses consciousness. **Never given an unconscious child anything by mouth.**

Hyperglycaemia

Hyperglycaemia ('a hyper') occurs when the blood sugar level is too high. It occurs slowly.

It is caused by too little insulin, illness or infection. Signs are similar to those before diagnosis of diabetes – thirst, passing large amounts of urine, sleepiness, pear drop smell to breath. Care of child: medical help and insulin injection are urgently needed to prevent unconsciousness.

It is important to inform the parents if their child has either of the above attacks.

FAILURE TO THRIVE

Growth is a major factor in determining a child's health. It is measured in terms of:

- weight
- height
- head circumference.

These measurements are plotted on **percentile charts** (growth charts), which are special graphs containing lines of growth worked out scientifically. The percentile charts on page 118 show, among others, the 2nd, 50th and 98th percentile lines. Measurements may fall on, or anywhere in between, a percentile line. The 50th line is average. Most children's growth curves fall between the 2nd and 98th percentile lines. Children whose measurements are outside these lines (especially below the 2nd percentile line) are usually referred to a specialist for investigation. In general, Asian children are smaller and lighter and children of Afro-Caribbean origin are taller and heavier than British white children.

Accurate measurements at birth are essential and should be followed by regular height and weight checks in infancy and childhood so that a picture of individual growth is built up. Head circumference is measured up to 2 years (or longer if there is any concern). When there is deviation from normal growth, such as failure to gain weight or weight loss over a period of time or zig-zagging over lines, referral to a specialist is indicated.

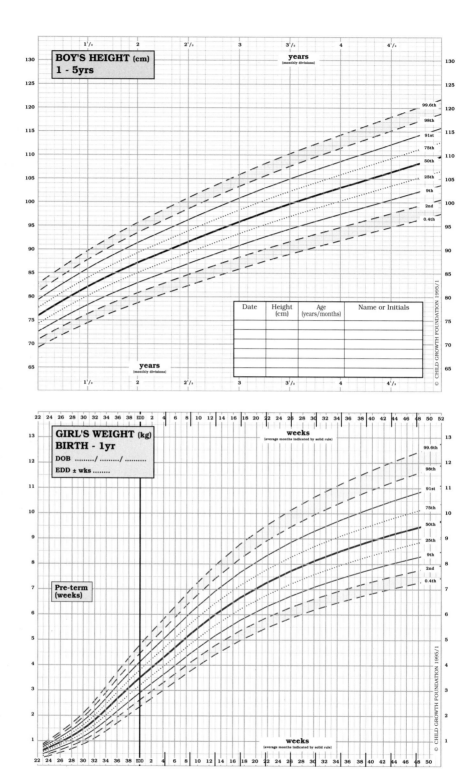

Examples of percentile charts

'Failure to thrive' refers to a young child who fails to grow. It particularly describes a child under 2 years who fails to gain weight. There may also be developmental delay, listlessness and apathy. Sometimes, it is due to medical reasons but most commonly the cause is under-nutrition, either because insufficient food is being offered or because there is a problem with feeding.

Failure to thrive may occur because of:

■ difficulty with sucking, for example poor technique, or cleft lip/palate
■ disorders of metabolism and poor absorption, allergies and intolerances (see above and also Chapter 6)
■ kidney and intestinal disorders, congenital heart disease, severe asthma or any other disorder which causes breathlessness and makes feeding difficult
■ poor quality child care for any of the following reasons:
  – insufficient or incorrectly made up feeds, over-dilute formula feeds
  – lack of warmth – cold environment, inadequate clothing – calories from food used to keep warm instead of to put on weight
  – difficult mother–child relationship, emotional and social stress in the family. Mother may be unresponsive to, or unaware of, her child's needs, may have a physical or emotional disability or suffer from post natal depression or other depressive illness. She may also lack support for her own needs
  – child abuse/neglect, deprivation of food
  – inappropriate diets – some children receive inappropriate diets because the parents/carers apply the principles of a high-fibre/low-fat diet, recommended for adult health, when feeding their children. This type of diet will not provide children with sufficient calories for growth and energy requirements and essential minerals and vitamins may be missing or poorly absorbed
■ poverty, poor budgeting and generally poor diet
■ lack of cooking facilities in hostel accommodation and reliance on convenience foods

Care for the child and family includes:

■ treatment of any medical problem or disorder
■ examination and observation of child, details of feeding pattern, growth measurements
■ health visitor support in parenting and possible referral to other support agencies
■ day care provision for the child
■ possible admission to hospital for assessment – if there is no medical reason for failure to thrive, the child will quickly start to gain weight, as the chart on page 120 shows
■ continued help and support for the family when the child returns home
■ regular measurements of growth and medical supervision for the child.

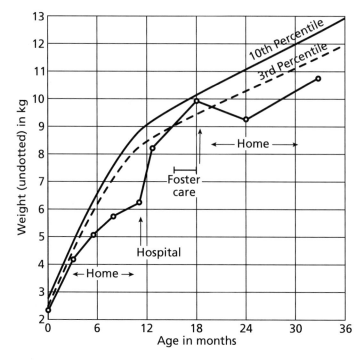

A percentile chart showing how a child's weight might change during stays in hospital, foster care and at home

QUICK CHECK

1 Which professionals are involved in working out special diets for children?
2 How might obesity affect:
   a) a baby's physical development?
   b) a child's emotional development?
3 What are the possible causes of overweight/obesity in infancy?
4 What practical measures could you take to prevent overweight/obesity in infancy?
5 What might be the effects of dental extractions on a pre-school child?
6 a) How does the mineral fluoride guard against tooth decay?
   b) What are the dangers to the teeth of too much fluoride?
7 a) What may lead you to think a child in your care is anaemic?
   b) If the child ate a vegetarian diet, how would you ensure her intake of dietary iron was being effectively absorbed?
8 What sensible dietary principles would you follow to prevent, as far as possible, constipation in children?
9 What do you understand by toddler diarrhoea?

10 a) What is the best source of vitamin D?
    b) When might infants be particularly at risk from vitamin D deficiency?
11 a) Name the condition caused by gluten intolerance?
    b) What are the typical signs of this disorder?
    c) What is the main dietary treatment?
12 a) Which two body systems are affected by cystic fibrosis?
    b) What are the symptoms?
    c) Describe the dietary treatment.
13 a) Name the blood test used to diagnose phenylketonuria.
    b) What are the main principles of dietary treatment for this disorder?
14 a) Describe the signs and symptoms leading to a diagnosis of diabetes.
    b) How would recognise hypoglycaemia and hyperglycaemia in a child with diabetes?
    c) What two items should a child with diabetes always carry with them?
15 a) How might poor quality child care result in failure to thrive?
    b) What support and care can be offered to the child and family?

KEY WORDS AND TERMS

You need to know what these words and phrases mean. Go back through the chapter and find out.

obesity	pancreatic enzyme
fluoride	phenylalanine
haemoglobin	Guthrie Test
haem iron and non-haem iron	insulin
rickets	hypoglycaemia
scurvy	hyperglycaemia
gluten	failure to thrive

9 *PARTICULAR EATING PRACTICES*

> **This chapter covers:**
> ■ **Multi-cultural diets**
> ■ **Vegetarian, vegan and other diets**

Multi-cultural diets

Increasingly children are enjoying a wide variety of foods and ingredients from different cultural backgrounds. What were once 'exotic' foods, such as avocados, mangoes, pineapples, pizza, spaghetti, kebabs and curries, are now readily available in supermarkets and family kitchens. So even children who are attending schools or nurseries in more remote areas in the UK have access to interesting diets.

THE ADVANTAGES OF A MULTI-CULTURAL APPROACH TO DIET

These include the following:
■ Children develop an awareness of and interest in other cultures.
■ Multi-ethnic foods often use less processed ingredients in their recipes and, as a result, are more natural.
■ Fruits are commonly used for desserts in many countries and there is less reliance on saturated fats, salty and sugary foods.
■ Offering foods from different cultures on school and nursery menus can promote self-respect in children from a variety of ethnic backgrounds, showing them that their culture is valued.
■ Children new to eating away from home will feel more secure when a familiar link – food – is provided.
■ Different tastes, textures and flavours enhance everyone's enjoyment and experience of food.

Child care workers have a professional responsibility to support parents/carers in their decisions over special eating practices for their children, whether this is for religious, moral or health reasons.

Multi-ethnic foods often use less processed ingredients in their recipes

RELIGIOUS ASPECTS OF FOODS

Some dietary restrictions are closely linked to religion (see Table 9.1, pages 128–9) but how closely these are followed will vary from one religious (or cultural) group to another. Some groups will ignore them completely and others will adhere totally. It is important to find out family policy and not make assumptions. For example, do not assume that all Asian children like rice.

REMEMBER!

- Many cultural groups will have periods of fasting, although children are usually exempt. Often a family meal will have been eaten during night time, for example during Ramadan, and children may be tired the following day.
- Always check with parents/carers about the special religious and cultural needs of any individual child.

CHANGES IN CULTURAL DIETS

Many diets of families from ethnic minority groups are now a combination of traditional and British foods. School-age children eat with and are influenced by their friends. British convenience foods are frequently advertised, easily available and cheap.

However, local shops selling Indian or Caribbean foods, for example, generally offer limited choices and may be more expensive. Families may have to travel further afield to obtain their own cultural foods, and this becomes especially difficult where there are only small groups of people wanting very special ethnic ingredients in their diets.

Children eating the Asian way – traditionally only the right hand is used to scoop up the food

Activities

1 Visit your nearest shop selling ethnic foods. Consider the variety of foods offered, including staples such as flours and rices.
   a) Are the foods offered especially 'healthy', for example whole-grain, brown rices, less processing in flours, etc?
   b) What would be the nutritional benefits of promoting these foods in a nursery?
   c) Look at the fruit and vegetables on display. Are there foods that are new to you? Research their particular nutritional values.
   d) Create a nursery menu for one week using dietary principles from a chosen ethnic group.
2 Many cultures have different ways of eating.
   a) Research the 'tools' used at mealtimes and the ages at which children are encouraged to use them.
   b) What cultures rarely use anything other than hands to eat?

Vegetarian, vegan and other diets

■ **Vegetarian** – not eating flesh (meat or fish)
■ **Vegan** – not eating foods of animal origin (including meat, fish and dairy products).

Interest in vegetarian diets has increased during recent years. The reasons may be health, cultural or moral. In young children the decision not to eat meat is taken for them by their parents/carers as the providers of their food. A vegetarian diet can provide all the nutrients for a child's growth and development, but as in any diet variety and balance is needed.

A vegan diet may present more challenges in ensuring healthy growth and development takes place. A mixture of plant proteins derived from cereals, peas, beans and nuts will provide sufficient good quality protein. However special care is needed to ensure that enough energy, calcium, iron and vitamins B and D are available. Dietary advice from a paediatric dietician may be required.

NUTRIENTS IN VEGETARIAN AND VEGAN DIETS

Protein
Milk and milk products are rich in protein as well as pulses, nuts and seeds. In addition bread, cereals and potatoes are useful. Remember, however, that only animal source proteins contain all the essential amino acids (HBV), and plant proteins only contain a selection (LBV).

It is esssential, therefore, that variety is provided if animal sources are not included in the diet – this allows for the deficits in one plant protein to be compensated for by the amino acids in another, for example rice and bean casserole, and baked beans on wholemeal toast. These meals then contain HBV proteins. This is known as complementation of plant proteins.

Look back at Chapter 2, page 10, to remind yourself about high and low biological value protein (HBV and LBV).

Iron
Meat and meat products are important sources of iron, an area where children may be deficient. In a vegetarian diet it is therefore essential to include in the diet helpings of lentils, leafy green vegetables (such a spinach), dried fruits, peas, beans or tofu, accompanied by a source of vitamin C (orange or citrus fruit drink) to increase absorption of iron.

Calcium
Milk and milk products are excellent sources of calcium and to a lesser extent so are leafy green vegetables, apricots, sesame seeds and bread. However calcium from plant foods may be more difficult to absorb from the intestine.

Vitamin D
This is found naturally in a limited number of foods, all of animal origin. Oily fish is an exceptionally valuable source, so if fish is excluded from the diet children need to take their pint of whole milk daily and eat other

sources where vitmains are added, such as breakfast cereals. Sunlight on the skin is the main source of vitamin D and very young children may need a supplement if exposure is limited.

Vitamin B$_{12}$

Milk and milk products are excellent sources of vitamin B$_{12}$, which is not found naturally in plant foods. However, breakfast cereals and yeast extract are fortified with this vitamin. Vegans will need to include a supplement to their diet.

Dietary fibre

Vegetarian diets potentially have a high fibre content which is not always suitable for growing children (see Chapter 3).

REMEMBER!

- A high fibre content may impair the absorption of minerals. Extra bran must not be given.
- When planning vegetarian diets look for 'hidden' animal products, for example stocks in soups, gravies, etc.

The chart on page 127 will help you with planning vegetarian and vegan diets.

OTHER DIETS

Zen macrobiotic diets

These diets are based on unrefined cereals and frequently exclude or limit vegetables and fruits. Fluid intake is also restricted. No particular food is actually forbidden

Fructarian diets

These diets are based on fruit and fermented, but uncooked, cereals and seeds.

SAFE PRACTICE

Both Zen macrobiotic and fructarian diets are nutritionally inadequate to support normal growth in young children and should be discouraged. Protein, energy malnutrition, anaemia and vitamin deficiency have been reported in children who have been placed on such diets.

PLANNING A VEGETARIAN DIET using four food groups, and fats and oils in moderation

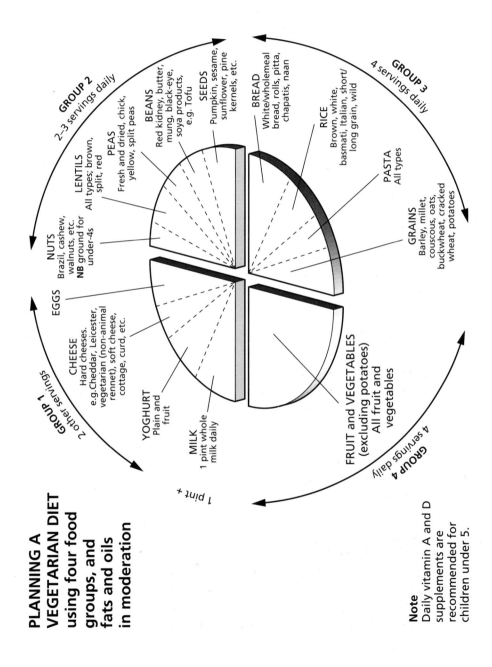

Vegans
- Exclude group 1 – additonal B$_{12}$ supplements necessary.
- Portions from remaining three sections will require adjustment.
- Dietary advice will be needed.

GROUP 2
2–3 servings daily

NUTS
Brazil, cashew, walnuts, etc. **NB** ground for under-4s

LENTILS
All types; brown, split, red

PEAS
Fresh and dried, chick, yellow, split peas

BEANS
Red kidney, butter, mung, black-eye, soya products, e.g. Tofu

SEEDS
Pumpkin, sesame, sunflower, pine kernels, etc.

GROUP 3
4 servings daily

BREAD
White/wholemeal bread, rolls, pitta, chapatis, naan

RICE
Brown, white, basmati, Italian, short/long grain, wild

PASTA
All types

GRAINS
Barley, millet, couscous, oats, buckwheat, cracked wheat, potatoes

GROUP 1
2 other servings

EGGS

CHEESE
Hard cheeses. e.g.Cheddar, Leicester, vegetarian (non-animal rennet), soft cheese, cottage, curd, etc.

YOGHURT
Plain and fruit

MILK
1 pint whole milk daily

GROUP 4
4 servings daily

FRUIT and VEGETABLES
(excluding potatoes)
All fruit and vegetables

1 pint +

Note
Daily vitamin A and D supplements are recommended for children under 5.

Table 9.1 The dietary principles and practices of different religions

Religion	Dietary principles and practices	Forbidden	Fasting
Hinduism	Hindus believe that all living things are sacred and it is considered wrong to take another creature's life to sustain one's own. The cow is sacred. Devout Hindus are therefore vegetarian (eating no meat, fish or eggs)	Beef Alcohol	Often adults, normally women, fast for one or two days per week, often restricting food intake rather than complete abstention.
Sikhism	As Hinduism		
Islam	These are laid down in the Muslim holy book, the Qur'an, and are regarded as the direct command of God. Meat must be *halal* (bled to death and dedicated to God by a Muslim present at the killing).	Pork and pork products Alcohol	All healthy adults must fast during the 30 days of Ramadan, eating and drinking nothing between dawn and sunset. The time of Ramadan changes with the calendar.
Judaism	Devout Jews adhere to the Jewish *kashrut* (dietary laws) as part of a code of discipline. Meat must be killed by the *kosher* method (the throat of a healthy animal or bird is cut quickly and the blood drained). The meat is then salted and steeped in water to remove all remaining blood. For the most orthodox Jews, meat and milk may not be used together in cooking and must be kept separate during preparation.	Pork and pork products Shellfish and any fish without fins or scales. All foods containing yeast during Passover (March or April).	Devout Jews take no food or liquid for 25 hours at the feast of Yom Kippur (the Day of Atonement) in September or October.

(continued)

Table 9.1 The dietary principles and practices of different religions *continued*

Religion	Dietary principles and practices	Forbidden	Fasting
Rastafarianism	Diet is very important. Rastafarians consider that the foods eaten reflect the health of the body and soul, and so only eat 'pure' foods. Additives and preservatives are avoided, canning of foods is thought to remove goodness, but frozen foods are acceptable. Most Rastafarians are vegetarian. They often prefer to eat in private.	Pork (some Rastafarians do eat other meat).	No specified times.

Note
Many Christian groups follow certain dietary restrictions at specified times. Sweet and rich foods are often given up during Lent. Buddhists sometimes refrain from eating meat on the days of the full and new moons.

QUICK CHECK

1 Why may multi-ethnic diets be 'healthier'?
2 List five commonly used foods that originate from the following countries/continents:
   a) Greece
   b) Italy
   c) India
   d) Africa
   e) China.
3 Which religions regularly have a fasting period?
4 How must meat be slaughtered to comply with the Jewish religious traditions?
5 How can you ensure that children who are eating a vegetarian diet receive their necessary energy and high biological protein intake?
6 In what ways could you introduce iron into a child's diet if he or she is restricted from eating red meat?
7 What foods are forbidden during the Jewish Passover?
8 A child who is vegetarian no longer 'likes' milk or cheese. What foods could supply the missing nutrients?
9 What arguments could you suggest to help a 6-year-old child who is vegetarian and who is being encouraged by her friends to try a beefburger?
10 Why are Zen macrobiotic and fructarian diets unsuitable for young children?
11 Which foods are forbidden to devout Hindus?
12 Describe Jewish *kashrut*.
13 What do you understand by the term 'pure' food for Rastafarians?
14 Which micro nutrients might be missing from a vegan diet?
15 What is Ramadan?

KEY WORDS AND TERMS

You need to know what these words and phrases mean. Go back through the chapter and find out.

Ramadan
halal
kosher
vegetarian

vegan
complementation in plant proteins
Zen macrobiotic
fructarian

---

10 COOKING WITH CHILDREN

> **This chapter covers:**
> ■ **The value of cooking**
> ■ **Organisation and management**

The value of cooking

Young children enjoy being involved in household tasks and imitating their carers, so cooking activities are usually very popular with them and can provide an ideal link between home and nursery. With increasing family pressures, more mothers working outside the home, and greater use of convenience foods, the opportunities for children to cook at home are often limited. Day nurseries, nursery classes and schools can provide children with a variety of cooking experiences in a safe and supervised setting.

Cooking activities enhance many developmental skills and offer a wide range of learning opportunities for children.

DEVELOPMENTAL AND LEARNING BENEFITS OF COOKING

Physical development
Gross motor skills and muscle power develop through beating, kneading and mixing. Manipulative skills improve when chopping, cutting, coring, slicing and stirring food. Pouring without spilling and separating egg yolk from the white extends hand–eye co-ordination.

Intellectual development
Science and maths are major areas of learning which can be introduced and built upon during cooking. Science concepts are learnt by 'doing'. Children can, for example, see the effects of heat and cold on food and liquid, how fats change into oil, how jelly and sugars dissolve when heated, and what happens to water when it is frozen. They can learn about dissolving, solutions and fermentation. They can begin to anticipate what will happen, for example, 'What will happen if the butter is heated?' or 'What will happen if more water is added?' Children can be encouraged to make decisions, predict outcomes and solve problems.

Weighing and measuring at home

How many cake cases to fill the baking sheet?

Introduction to maths occurs in endless ways – counting, measuring, sorting, grading, fractions and area. Children can learn about weight and the different amounts achieved from similar weights, for example 1 g fat compared with 1 g flour. They see an egg increase in bulk when beaten and how cake and bread mixtures rise and increase in size when baked in the oven. Preparing and using the ingredients according to the recipe teaches the children about sequencing and develops an awareness of time.

Other learning includes talking about where different foods come from and how they grow, cooking and eating foods from a variety of cultures and countries as well as menu planning and shopping and counting change. How to use and care for cooking and eating utensils and specialist equipment, such as weighing scales and cake tins, is also part of the learning experience.

Sensory development

All the senses are stimulated during cooking activities. Children can **see** the colour, size, shape and amount of the various foods and how they are often changed by the application of heat. They can **feel** the different textures (rough, smooth, lumpy, etc.) and **hear** the boiling, sizzling, crunching and whisking as food is prepared or eaten. The **taste** of sweet, sour, bitter and smooth foods always promotes much discussion and interest and the variety of **smells** can be an important link with their kitchen at home.

This extension of sensory experience is particularly important and beneficial for children with vision or hearing impairment.

Language development

Commentary and interaction while cooking takes place will introduce many new words. Younger children can extend their vocabulary with words such as more, less, balance, light, heavy, melting, thick, thin, etc., while older children will learn more technical words such as sediment, solution and fermentation. Adult interaction is important in the naming of cooking utensils and describing processes.

Emotional development

Creating an end product provides a great sense of achievement satisfaction and fun, especially if a tummy is filled in the process!

The necessary kneading and pummelling of dough can provide a healthy outlet for the release of tension, especially perhaps on a wet day when no outdoor play is possible. Rolling and manipulating pastry can be relaxing.

Activities can go wrong – cakes burn or fail to rise. So the adult will need to be flexible in managing disappointments.

Social development

The children learn to co-operate and work towards a common goal. This involves team work, sharing and taking turns. Patience is needed when waiting for cooking to be completed, for a jelly to set or for dough to rise. Then there is the group discipline and responsibility of washing up and tidying away, followed by the pleasure of sharing food with peers.

PROMOTION OF HEALTH

Early cooking can lay the foundation for a life-long healthy attitude to food. Valuable skills such as bread and 'light' pastry making will always be useful for both boys and girls.

The involved adult at cooking time

The quality of the learning experience will depend, to a large extent, on your ability to explain, question and answer the children as the cooking takes place.

Organisation and management

Planning and organisation are vital and safety must be paramount. Not more than four children under 5 years, or six children between 5 and 7 years, should take part in a cooking activity with one adult. The children not involved in cooking will need a different activity so they are not getting in the way and posing a possible safety hazard. It is a good idea to list children not involved so they can have a chance next time.

PLANNING

Decide what you wish to cook and make a list of the developmental skills and areas of language you hope to extend. Keep this list for future reference. For example, making sandwiches is useful pre-maths work, with quarters and halves of bread. Hot cross buns link with science concepts of fermentation and the effects of heat. The cooking can perhaps link into a wider school or nursery theme, such as a project on 'Warm Climates' which could mean shopping in a street market for ingredients for an exotic fruit salad, or colourful ratatouille. Children can make lists for the shopping.

Consider the parents'/carers' cultural and moral wishes regarding food for their child, both in handling and eating food. Consider fillings for sandwiches, for example ham would be unsuitable for children who are Muslim, Jewish or vegetarian

Activity
What dishes could be prepared in the following circumstances:
a) no source of heat?
b) boiling water only?
c) hot plate only?
d) full oven facilities?

Developmental considerations

The age and skill level of the group must be considered:

- **Nursery: 2–4-year-olds**

  Plan for limited concentration – waiting for bread to rise, cakes to cook or jelly to set may be difficult, at this age and quicker results will be required. Physical strength for pouring and beating will be limited.

- **Nursery school/Reception class: 4–6-year-olds**

  At this age more sophisticated concepts can be introduced. Children can now wait for the transition of a cake mix into a sponge or the chopped vegetables into soup.

- **Infant/Junior: 6–8-year-olds**

  Children will now be able to follow a recipe card with simple written, or pictorial instructions. Concepts of fermentation in bread-making and the extended process of two proving periods would now be tolerated. The cooking activity can link in with work on the National Curriculum in Maths, Science, History, Geography and English at Key stages 1 and 2.

- **Children with special needs**

  Consider whether adaptations are needed – wheelchair access to the cooking area, modifications to equipment and large print recipe cards. Will you need additional help? Perhaps a parent could be invited in for the cooking session?

  The chart opposite summarises all the points you will need to consider when planning a cooking session.

Preparation of the children

- Discuss the reasons for a chosen recipe. Involve them in the planning, for example by reading books to discover the origin of unfamiliar ingredients.
- Explain the safety rules clearly and fully.
- Ensure their hands are washed, nails short, no rings, hair tied back and clean aprons. Explain that they should not taste food without your permission, nor should they eat food that has fallen onto the floor.
- For maximum fun and learning, everyone must be involved and 'doing', not just observing, so sufficient equipment, bowls, spoons, aprons, etc. for each child will be needed.
- Children could do their own measuring, counting and weighing, working from recipe cards they have been involved in designing.

GOOD PRACTICE

- Is there equal access for both genders in your planning?
- Is there a 'healthy eating' message in your recipe?
- Is there a realistic savoury and sweet balance in your recipes?
- Are you introducing foods from different cultures?

1 CAN YOU ACTUALLY COOK WHAT YOU ARE ASKING THE CHILDREN TO COOK?
If you have never used yeast before and plan to make rolls, a practice run is advisable.

2 HOW LONG WILL THE SESSION TAKE?
Hours? Several days? – This may be so, if shopping with the children is involved.

3 WILL THE CHILDREN BE ABLE TO TASTE THEIR 'WORK' BEFORE THEY GO HOME?
Check the cooking and cooling down time. Children will be very disappointed at not seeing, smelling and tasting their results before home time.

PERSONAL PREPARATION
↓
THINK!

8 ARE THERE HYGIENE FACILITIES?
You will need facilities for hand-washing and clearing up.

4 HOW MUCH WILL THE ACTIVITY COST?
- Is the cost realistic?
- Who will meet the cost?

7 IS THERE ADEQUATE SPACE?
Check where you will be carrying out the activity. Make sure there is adequate room and that the area can be cleaned for food preparation

6 IS THE EQUIPMENT YOU NEED AVAILABLE?
- Cooker or hotplate
- Kettle
- Pots and pans,cooling tray
- Scales
- Bowls
- Sieves
- Utensils
- Access to a refrigerator
The availability and variety of equipment will influence your choice of activity.

5 WHAT INGREDIENTS WILL BE NEEDED?
- Make sure the foods you need are readily available.
- If they are fresh foods, how far in advance will you buy them and where will you store them?

- Are you using a variety of flavours, tastes, textures and smells?
- Provide encouragement and support
- Praise efforts
- Take time to explain and interact
- Observe reactions
- Remind about 'independent tasting'

THE COOKING SESSION

Liaison with the nursery team will be necessary as cooking may need to be undertaken with several groups over a period of days so that no child is left out.
- With your group, collect all the ingredients and equipment needed.
- Ensure your cooking area is clean and free of clutter.
- If an oven or other source of heat is to be used, check the safety procedures and remind the group of the rules.

How many pastry rounds from one large circle?

- Supervise weighing and measuring, both for accuracy and to reinforce counting and measuring concepts.
- Ensure that all the children see the different stages taking place – 'rubbing in' when making pastry, the stages of elasticity in bread dough and the proving process, the effects of liquid on dry ingredients and how quickly the jelly melts with varying temperatures.
- Teach the children to use equipment correctly – how to cut with sharp knives, use peelers and beaters, how to estimate timings on a microwave oven. These are all useful life skills.

SAFE PRACTICE

Whenever heat is used in a cooking activity you will need to decide what is safe for children to do.

- The use of hot fat and frying are unsuitable activities for young children.
- An adult can open an oven to let a child place her cooking inside, but the child **must** be protected with oven gloves.
- Children should not be allowed to light a gas oven with matches. They may, under supervision, operate a gas oven with automatic ignition or an electric oven.
- Pouring boiling water requires muscle power and co-ordination and mishaps can be serious. Adults must always undertake this task.

Teaching children how to keep safe in a potentially dangerous area like the kitchen is an important aspect of any cooking activity.

- Encourage follow-up activities, science tasks, story/songs linking to curriculum projects, such as food sources, food chains, growing food.

FOLLOW-UP WORK

Everyone needs to be involved in the clearing away and washing up. Think what you are going to do with the food that has been prepared/cooked? Suggestions might include:

■ letting the children take the food home if suitable containers are available
■ laying the food out on a prepared table and making a special occasion of it for all the children in the nursery or class
■ setting up a shop in the home corner (decide on your 'currency')
■ inviting parents/carers to see and taste the results of the children's work.

SELF-EVALUATION

■ Do you consider that the session went well?
■ What changes, if any, would you arrange for another occasion?
■ Did you manage to involve all the children and did they participate fully?
■ How accurate was your timing?
■ Did you extend all areas of the learning process? Look at your skills and language check list.
■ How could you assess whether the children remembered what they learnt in the session and how could you reinforce the learning?
■ Make a list of the new words you felt were introduced to the children, by you, during the activity.
■ Did another worker observe the session? Did he or she have additional comments that would help your personal assessment?

Finally, keep the recipe in a resource file for the nursery or class, adding any comments and amendments for future use.

Activity
a) Research a variety of different religious festivals.
   What special foods are offered during these occasions?
b) After liaison and discussion with the nursery staff, plan and implement an activity to cook one of these foods. You will need to prepare the children about the background and reasons for the foods being prepared. How will you do this? Would it be appropriate to involve parents/carers who have special knowledge of the festival foods and their traditions?
   Remember the developmental stage of the group.
c) Prepare your menu cards.
d) Take your group out to buy the necessary ingredients.

QUICK CHECK

1 What gross and fine motor skills can children gain from cooking?
2 Describe the science concepts that can be introduced during a bread-making session.
3 What possible outcomes or predictions could you pose to a child when making jelly?
4 How might you introduce maths when making sandwiches?
5 How could you develop sensory awareness when cooking with children with special needs?
6 List 20 new words associated with cake making that you could introduce.
7 How can cooking lay the foundation for a healthy attitude to food?
8 How could you best meet the different developmental needs of two groups of children, one aged 4 and the other 6 years, when planning a cooking activity?
9 What cooking activity might you offer to a child with a visual impairment?
10 How could you reflect a multi-cultural approach to cooking with young children?
11 Why is it important for all children to be involved and not just observing when cooking?
12 What safety factors are essential when using an oven with a group of children?
13 List the plans you would make for a cake-making session with a group of three 3–year-olds.
14 What social development can take place during a group cooking activity?
15 Why is it important to check the gender balance of children involved in cooking sessions?

KEY WORDS AND TERMS

You need to know what these words and phrases mean. Go back through the chapter and find out.

science and maths concepts   stimulation of all the senses

GLOSSARY OF NUTRITIONAL TERMS

Allergy   A severe reaction to a particular food

Amino acids   The chemical structure of proteins – compounds of carbon, hydrogen, oxygen and nitrogen

Colostrum   The first important milk produced by the breasts, rich in protein and antibodies

COMA   Committee on Medical Aspects of Food Policy

Curd-dominant formula milk   Baby milk containing the protein casein, for the hungrier baby

Dairy foods   Milk, butter, cheese, cream, yoghurt

Dehydration   Loss of water from body or food

Dietary reference values   Recommended nutrient requirements for different groups of individuals

E numbers   Numbers given to food additives approved by the European Union (EU)

Empty calories   Energy obtained from single nutrient foods, particularly sugars, sugary foods and drinks

Energy   Essential fuel for all body processes

Enzymes   Special proteins needed for all chemical reactions in the body

Fluoride   A trace element which protects tooth enamel

Food groups   Foods grouped according to their main nutrient content

Fore milk   The milk at the beginning of a breast feed which is high in lactose

Fortified foods   Foods which have vitamins and minerals added

Gluten   A protein found in cereals such as wheat, barley, oats and rye

Glycogen   The name given to glucose stored in the liver and muscles

Haem iron   The most readily absorbed dietary iron

Haemoglobin   A protein in red blood cells which carries oxygen around the body

Halal   Meat from animals slaughtered according to Islamic (Muslim) religion

High biological value (HBV)   Proteins found in animal foods and containing all the essential amino acids

Hind milk   The milk which follows the fore milk, rich in fat (calories)

Hydrolysed protein   A specially adapted formula milk used in allergy management

Insulin   A hormone produced by the pancreas necessary for carbohydrate metabolism

Intolerance   Inability to tolerate a certain food, usually short-lived. Signs and symptoms may include vomiting, diarrhoea, rashes and failure to thrive

Irradiation   A method of preserving food using gamma rays

Joule/calorie   Measurement of food energy

Kosher   Meat from animals slaughtered according to Judaism, the Jewish religion

Lactose   Milk sugar

Let-down reflex   The mechanism by which milk is squeezed out of the milk cells into the milk ducts

Low biological value (LBV)   Proteins found in vegetable and plant foods containing only some essential amino acids

Macronutrients   Nutrients which supply energy and are needed in large amounts – proteins, fat and carbohydrate

Metabolism   Describes all the changes that take place in the body to do with food and energy use

Micronutrients   Nutrients needed in small amounts – vitamins and minerals, which do not supply energy

Moulds   Invisible tiny plants on food surfaces which cause food spoilage

Non-haem iron   The less well-absorbed dietary iron

Nutrients   The building blocks of food, which provide material for growth and maintain good health

Pancreatic enzyme   A digestive juice produced by the pancreas. It can be manufactured artificially

Pathogens   Harmful organisms

Phenylalanine   An essential amino acid

Polyunsaturated fat   Fat, mainly from vegetable/plant sources – may lower level of blood cholesterol

Preservatives   Natural or artificial additives used to prolong the life of food

Protein   A macronutrient essential for growth and repair of body tissue, can be animal or plant source

Protein complementation   Combining a variety of LBV protein foods to ensure all essential amino acids are obtained

Saturated fat   Fat, mainly from animal sources, linked to coronary heart disease

Soya milk   Milk produced from the soya bean

Staple foods   Foods which form the bulk of a diet

Tartrazine   An orange colouring added to sweets and drinks

Toxins/toxic   Poisons/poisonous

Unavailable carbohydrate   The term used to describe fibre – carbohydrate that cannot be used by the body

Vegan   A diet that excludes the eating of animal flesh and products

Vegetarian   A diet that excludes the eating of animal flesh

Well-balanced diet   A daily diet which includes a wide variety of foods from the food groups

Whey-dominant formula milk   Baby milk nearest in composition to breast milk, containing the protein lactalbumin

Yeasts   Micro organsims that can cause food spoilage but are used in fermentation, for example in breads and alcohol

USEFUL ADDRESSES

British Diabetic Association
10 Queen Anne Street
London
W1M 0BD

Child Growth Foundation
2 Mayfield Avenue
Chiswick
London
W4 1PW

Child Poverty Action Group
4th floor
1–5 Bath Street
London
EC1V 9PY

Coeliac Society
PO Box 220
High Wycombe
Bucks
HP11 2HY

Cystic Fibrosis Research Trust
Alexandra House
5 Blyth Road
Bromley
Kent
BR1 3RS

Food Commission
102 Gloucester Place
London
W1H 3DA

Food Safety Directorate
Ministry of Agriculture, Fisheries and Food
London
SE99 7TT

Food Standards Division
Ministry of Agriculture, Fisheries and Food
Nobel House
17 Smith Square
London
SW1P 3JR
(for information on food labelling)

National Society for Phenylketonuria and Allied Disorders Ltd
26 Towngate Grove
Mirfield
West Yorkshire
WF14 9JF

NCH Action for Children
Policy and Information Department
85 Highbury Park
London
N5 1UD

School Meals Campaign
PO Box 402
London WC1H 9TZ

SCOPE
12 Park Crescent
London
S1N 4EQ

Vegan Society
7 Battle Road
St Leonards-on-Sea
East Sussex
PN37 7AA

Vegetarian Society
Parkdale
Dunham Road
Altrincham
Cheshire
WA14 4QG

INDEX

Page references in **bold** indicate tables or charts, those in *italics* illustrations.

media   81–2
metabolism   4
micronutrients   2, *2*, 3
microwave ovens   57
milk   34
   see also breast-feeding; formula milk
milk protein allergy   86
minerals   2, 14, 15, **22, 26–7**
Montgomery's tubercules   48
moulds   89
multi-cultural diets   122–6

NACNE (National Advisory Committee
   on Nutrition Education)   4
niacin   **24**, 84, **112**
nipples   48, *49*, 51, **53**
non-haem iron   108
nutrients   2, *2*, 3–4
   cheap sources of   84
   dairy, staple and fortified foods
      17
   food groups   16
   role of essential nutrients   10–15,
      18–27
   vegetarian and vegan diets
      127–8
nutrition, definition   1
nuts   *13*, 37

obesity   102–4
oils   15, **18**, 33
overfeeding of infants   **65**
overweight   102–4

packed lunches   79–80, *80*
pancreatic enzyme   115
pathogens   89, 90
peanut allergy   37
pellagra   **112**
percentile charts   117, *118, 120*
peristalsis   6
phenylalanine   115
phenylketonuria (PKU)   115
phosphorus   **26**
plant protein   10, 125
poisoning, food   85
polyunsaturated fats   11, **18**, 33
portions, children's daily   38
possetting   **65**
potassium   **27**, 36
poverty   82
preconception
   dietary needs   43–4

pregnancy
   dietary needs   44–5
preservation of food   95–6
preservatives   86, 97, **98**
protein   2, 6, 10, 15, **17**, 32–3, 84
   in colostrum   50
   complementation   10, 125
pulses   *11*, 36
pyridoxine   **24**

Ramadan   **128**
Rastafarianism   **129**
religion and diet   123, **128–9**
retinol   **24**
riboflavin   **24**, 84
rickets   110, **112**
RNIs (Reference Nutrient Intakes)
   4, **8**

saliva   5
salt   14, **27**, 35, 36
saturated fats   11, **18**, 33
school meals   77–8
science   131
scurvy   **112**
seeds   *13*, 37
Sikhism   **128**
snacks   40, *41*, 43
sodium chloride   14, **27**, 35, 36
soya milk   55, 86
special diets   101
special needs children
   and cooking activities   136
   feeding   73–4
spina bifida   44
staple foods   16
starches   6, 12
sterilisation of feeding equipment
   56, *56*
stomach   5–6, *5*
sugars   6, 12, **19**, 35, 105, 116
supplements, dietary   37, 45
supply and demand breast-feeding
   49

tartrazine   86
tea   36
thiamin   **24**, 84
tocopherol *see* Vitamin E
toddlers, feeding   70–3, 74–5
tooth decay   **105**, 105–7
toxins   86, 89
trace elements   14, **21, 27**